My
Money
My Way

My Money My Way

Taking Back Control of Your Financial Life

Kumiko Love

PORTFOLIO / PENGUIN

Portfolio / Penguin
An imprint of Penguin Random House LLC
penguinrandomhouse.com

Most Portfolio books are available at a discount when purchased in
quantity for sales promotions or corporate use. Special editions, which include
personalized covers, excerpts, and corporate imprints, can be created when
purchased in large quantities. For more information, please call (212) 572-2232
or e-mail specialmarkets@penguinrandomhouse.com. Your local bookstore can
also assist with discounted bulk purchases using the Penguin Random
House corporate Business-to-Business program. For assistance in locating a
participating retailer, e-mail B2B@penguinrandomhouse.com.

ISBN 9780593418840 (hardcover)
ISBN 9780593418857 (ebook)

Printed in the United States of America
1st Printing

Book design by Alexis Farabaugh

To all of the women who have lost hope with their finances.
It's time to start a new journey. Your way.

Contents

Part One

Build a New Foundation

Make It Happen

Introduction and a Note
on Honoring Yourself

We women are forever telling ourselves two lies: that we're bad with money, and that we don't have anything to wear. While this book won't exactly help you with the latter—though Madewell jeans are 100 percent worth saving for—it *will* help you with your money goals like no book ever has before.

No more feeling out of control with your finances.

No more skyrocketing debt.

No more stress and anxiety and constant worry.

And—most important—*no more traditional budgeting.*

Traditional budgets fail because they focus exclusively on the numbers. Moreover, they're entirely too restrictive, anxiety producing, and disempowering: they leave us dependent on people out there who "know the secret." Despite all of the fancy step-by-step programs that purportedly break the "big" concepts down into specific "bite-sized" instructions, traditional budgeting still leaves you overwhelmed, confused, and unsure you're doing it right as you bend over backward to follow rules you don't understand. Worse, you feel resentful of being made to feel like a child who constantly has to slap herself on the wrist when she spends. And when all of that restricting results in failure? You'll berate yourself for your lack of discipline. ("What is wrong with me? Why can't I ever seem to get it together?")

But discipline alone is not enough. You need more discipline, and this book.

I'm Kumiko Love, founder of the leading personal finance website *The Budget Mom*, creator of the Budget by Paycheck Method, and an accredited financial counselor who helps millions of women around the world reinvent their money stories. And I take a different approach to money, one that actually relies very little on the numbers. Money is *never* a conversation about numbers. When we talk about money, we're talking about so much more than that. We're talking about emotional health. We're talking about happiness. We're talking about the quality of your life.

Your financial health is your emotional health—and that's something women aren't taught. We feel guilty about money, have trouble saving money, have issues asking for money, spend money when we feel good, spend money when we feel bad, don't know how to manage it, don't know what to do with it, don't know how much we have of it, and certainly don't know how much we need. And that's because so many of the decisions we make with our money are tied to how we feel about ourselves in any given moment of time. We spend money out of panic, fear, insecurity, low self-esteem, anxiety, doubt, shame, and all sorts of complex human emotions that, frankly, are really messing with our quality of life. *That's* what this book is about. Regardless of your income level or credit card balance, you deserve to live well. You deserve to save with dignity. And you deserve to spend money toward your own unique dreams.

That's what I call **my money, my way.**

And it's about what you DO need, more than what you shouldn't buy.

I can't tell you how many women I've seen drastically overcorrect their money habits by depriving themselves of joy. It breaks my heart to see people deny themselves because they are afraid of the financial consequences, because they aren't prepared, or—worst of all—because someone told them that particular experience was off limits: When a new mom shames herself for going out to eat with her friends because she "wasn't supposed to." When a person automatically assumes they can't afford to go back to school. When you don't ever buy organic because it's "for rich people."

That's not how we're going to live. Instead, we're going to manage our money—and, by extension, our lives—from a place of strength. We're going to start with asking what you need your money to *do* for you. How do you want your money to serve you? How can the act of budgeting be a way to honor yourself, rather than deny yourself?

If you're like, "Yeah, okay, Miko, try honoring my negative bank balance," I get it—this is the hard part (at least at first). But it isn't because you're bad with money, I promise. It's because you're operating under outdated and false assumptions about your money and the role it plays in your life.

Here's the thing: Financially anxious people don't know themselves, what they're aiming for, or what actually makes their lives full. They don't know what makes them happy. Consequently, they spend money on things and experiences out of a subconscious insecurity, out of a need to fit in or become someone else, or because they have no idea what really brings value to their lives. For example, when a woman gets her nails done every week because "all the other women" do—but she carries credit card debt because of it. Or when a student blows money on a concert to see a band she doesn't like because her friends are all going, and then the next week doesn't have money for books. They don't know what a life of freedom and abundance means to them because they haven't yet defined those things for themselves.

Until you know who you are, what you want, and how you desire to live your life, how could you possibly know how to manage your money?

This is what I'm going to teach you in *My Money My Way*. I won't be giving you a rigid set of rules about how much you can and can't spend at Starbucks (you don't need those); instead, I'm going to teach you how to think about money differently so you can make different decisions. You'll be making those decisions based on your very unique situation: your personal values, your driving emotions, your particular needs. Once you figure out that criteria, your financial plan will practically write itself.

It's not about deprivation, but desire. Because you are not the problem; shame is the problem. Guilt is the problem. Society's expectations are the problem. *You* are the solution.

I hope this book gives you the confidence to trust yourself. I hope this book gives you the bright, open heart to try again. And I hope this book makes you SHINE.

My
Money
My Way

CHAPTER ONE

The Ice Cream Cone
That Changed My Life

S ome couples fight about money, but my ex-husband and I had an even bigger problem: we didn't talk about it at all.

He would give me his paycheck and I would pay the bills, and while that might sound like we were Adults of the Year, what we really were was clueless. Plans? What were those? We were winging it daily, neither one of us caring enough about our finances to even have a conversation.

The day I got pregnant, however, we were finally forced to take a harder look at things. How were we going to afford a baby? I told myself we would make it work; we would find ways to be thrifty. I painted the nursery walls myself, a light green color, with paint I found in the clearance section at Home Depot. I watched DIY videos on YouTube and tutorials on Pinterest. I made bookshelves from old rain gutters and made all of the artwork for the baby's bedroom out of construction paper and Crayola markers. I was determined to create special memories with the little money we had. It would be fine; we would just wing it like we always did.

But then I actually *had* the baby.

If you've ever looked into the eyes of a newborn, you know it upends everything you thought about what matters. For the first time, "day by day" was not good enough. "Seat of my pants" was not good enough. My son, James, made me long for an all-new sense of stability, a life that was beautiful, intentional, safe, and designed.

Enter the moment I decided I needed a budget. A *real* one. Not the flimsy, just-for-decoration kind, but the kind that would actually help us strategically move forward as a family.

This sounded like a reasonable idea—you know, financial goals and all—until I realized my husband and I were on totally different teams. We had finally started talking about money, but every time we did, it would result in a fight. We never had any clear purpose or bigger ambitions. There I was, cycling through various types of budgeting methods, looking for one that would actually make us better with our money— from percentage based to monthly based and beyond—but by the end of each month, we would pay our bills on time but have nothing left over. It was a constant, never-ending struggle.

Soon, our debt became unmanageable. We had one or two credit cards totaling $6,000, and I had ballooning student loans, and medical bills from a severe motorcycle accident. But I still managed to make what little progress I could, taking advantage of balance transfers, filing for financial hardship with the hospital, and getting on an income-based repayment plan for my student loans. Eventually—with enough focus and discipline—I was able to pay it all off and was so incredibly proud.

I hadn't achieved everything I wanted, but I was getting by. I was making it work.

But then the divorce happened.

As a kid, I lived through my parents' separation, and it was one of the most defining moments of my youth. I remember the suffering it caused my mom. I watched as fear took over her life. The hurt I felt had ripple effects straight through to adulthood.

So when I found myself in the position of initiating my own divorce, all I felt was heart-clenching failure. To complicate matters, the logistics of it all were herculean: it was near impossible to find a place of my own with an annual income of only $30,000 from my job as an assistant in the finance industry. With a little luck, I *did* finally find an eight-hundred-square-foot apartment. For several months, it was mostly empty. I left my marriage with only a few bags of belongings, so we didn't have any furniture. I managed to buy a TV from Walmart with one of my paychecks, and we watched that TV nightly, eating our dinner on the living room floor. Divorce is complicated and difficult for many obvious reasons, but for me, the loneliness hit hard. When I was married, there was togetherness. Finances together, struggles together, stories together, dinners together. But then it was just me. It felt lonely, scary, and dark.

More than the loneliness, however, was the guilt. Even though I knew that this decision was best for our family, I also knew I had stripped away everything my son had known: a backyard, his own bedroom, his toys, the swing set. I was in a constant panic about how he was handling the new changes, and because of that panic, the problem compounded: I kept trying to live a life that wasn't mine. I wanted to pretend like everything was normal. I wanted to pretend like I still had it together, that nothing had changed. I wanted to give my son the life he deserved. And so out of a complex emotional cocktail of shame, guilt, and fear, one morning I woke up, took the day off work, and ordered brand-new furniture on my credit card.

A *lot* of furniture.

I was desperate to prove I was a good mom. So desperate, in fact, that I also decided to order some fresh new decor while I was at it (no more construction paper and Crayola for us)—not to mention a new microwave, pots and pans, ALL new kitchen gadgets, and a brand-new bed. Do you know how expensive *beds* are?

I'm sure it comes as no surprise that I immediately maxed out my limit. That's when I made the grand decision to start accepting credit card offers I received in the mail. I thought to myself, "I can pay this off over the next year, it's not a big deal." In my mind, it was about building a home my son loved and felt comfortable in, a safe and happy place. But, in reality, I was spending money I didn't have in order to feel like I was living up to my own standards of what I thought a good mom was.

The total damage from my "good mom binge" came to over $20,000 worth of crippling, high-interest debt. Coupled with the shiny new Jeep Patriot I brilliantly drove right off the lot right before my divorce, I soon found myself suddenly owing *seventy-eight thousand United States dollars*. There I was, still living day by day, still making frivolous financial decisions I rationalized as helpful ones.

Of course, I never thought I'd have my big moment of truth in a McDonald's drive-through.

We were at the park. My son wanted ice cream. We got in the car and drove to the closest McDonald's. I pulled up to the window and ordered one. I will never forget the price: $1.09. As I went to pay, I reached inside my wallet and pulled out my debit card, but then hesitated: I didn't even know if I had $1.09 in my checking account. So I took out my credit card instead. *I financed a $1.09 ice cream cone for my son.*

4

And suddenly, for the first time, I saw everything with intense, painful clarity.

As I looked back at him, happily licking away, I got *mad*. Sometimes, the truth will anger you, but it'll always be what saves you. In that moment I knew I was going to have to fight harder for a life he could be proud of that didn't involve shame, poverty, and the endless financial stress spiral I was putting us through. I wanted him to be able to experience life without the constant emotional struggle, to be able to actually *live*—or at least order an ice cream cone without being traumatized. I didn't want to model unhealthy behaviors. I didn't want him to feel the side effects of my less-than-stellar choices.

I was also tired of being endlessly preoccupied with money, never knowing how much I had in my checking account, constantly stressing, stressing, stressing, and never being present with him because my mind was always somewhere else.

This was one of those moments when you realize you no longer have a choice. Being financially successful went from being a "nice to have" to an urgent necessity. And the very first thing I knew I'd have to do?

Get serious about understanding money.

I needed to get serious about making it, strategizing it, planning it, and using it.

And I needed a real budget that worked.

It's not that I hadn't tried to make one work in the past; I *had* tried. But none of them seemed set up for living in the real world. And perhaps that's because I didn't know then what I know now: that budgeting isn't hard because of the budget, but because of the rules. Change the rules, change the outcome. I had a lot to learn.

In the meantime, however, I knew I needed to try *something*—anything. So I began to experiment. I scrapped what I thought I "should" do, and instead focused on what actually felt useful and helpful . . . for *me*. For example, instead of throwing every dollar toward my debt and eating nothing but rice and beans for three years—common wisdom in the budgeting world—I confronted my emotional spending head-on. I realized low self-esteem caused me to overspend, so instead of going to the mall when I felt low, I put on a pair of sneakers and went for a run. Little by little, I took note of where I was making progress and what didn't seem to work in the context of my life. And little by little, my new personal budgeting method—one that plucked the most useful ideas from traditional approaches and combined them into a new hybrid method that was aligned with *my* goals instead of everybody else's—was born.

And by the end of my experiment, I didn't just have a budget:

I had freedom and fulfillment.

I had hope again.

Here's the thing about budgeting that most people don't realize: It's not about money. It's about *you*. Budgeting is personal development in disguise.

If you know what you want from your money, progress can happen—no matter how much (or how little) of it you have. The thing is, most of us don't understand what we really want from our money.

When I was in that McDonald's parking lot all those years ago, I didn't know what *I* wanted. I was copying and pasting other people's goals into my life, assuming theirs were as good as any. It took years of experimentation, self-exploration, and asking myself hard questions to finally figure out that *I could want other things*. That I did want other things. And I needed to learn to use money as a tool to pursue my dreams instead of react to my fears.

The Ice Cream Cone That Changed My Life

Budgeting forces you to understand yourself in all-new ways because it asks you to decide what you want to actually accomplish with your money beyond simply "paying the bills." I had to define what success felt and looked like in my own life, and learn how to address the underlying issues of what was *really* causing my out-of-control spending. It wasn't because I desperately needed a new mirror from Target.

Every single day I looked at my son, and every single day my purpose became clearer. I started budgeting my money differently, doing it every time I got paid, and designed a physical budgeting calendar that allowed me to see my finances from a new perspective. Eventually I started using a zero-based budget—we'll talk more about that soon—which gave me the control I needed to allocate every dollar toward things that mattered to me and my life. Nothing was arbitrary. Every dollar was spoken for.

And *it worked.*

Press fast-foward on this story, and my life now is nothing like what it once was. I wouldn't have believed you if you'd told me that day in the McDonald's drive-through that in the future I'd be the Budget Mom, a world-renowned personal finance expert, blogger, and author who has millions of followers from all around the world. Or that I am finally in a place where I don't have to think about money. I spend time with my son every day. I'm able to send him to sports camps and social events when they come up. Last year, I took a gorgeous vacation with my mom. And most recently?

I paid for our brand-new home in cash.

This is the "happily ever after" part of what I call **Budget by Paycheck**, the name of the system I ultimately designed to help other women who have lost their way with their finances. My business and website are not only a business and blog: they're a community of women from around the world. And we're not just "budgeting"—we're building.

We're using our desires to design our money and take back control of our lives.

It might be difficult for you to envision a life you might never have experienced, one without the question of "Will I have enough?" constantly hanging over your head. One where you don't have to be afraid of emergencies. One where you can say with pride, "I know what I'm doing."

But trust me, if it was possible for a girl who was once so broke she had to decide whether to pay the rent or put food on the table, it's possible for you, too.

Inside these pages, I'm going to teach you how to view money as an engine instead of an enemy. The reason so many other financial programs get it wrong is that they focus on the *numbers* and miss what actually matters: you, your life, your family, and what makes you actually feel joyful, happy, confident, and free. Not just financially free, but truly free to live well.

Life > money. Having options is better than any dollar amount in your bank account. Spending time with your kids. Giving back to your family. Making unforgettable memories. Living without financial anxiety. Trusting in yourself. And being able to be present for the million moments that make up your day.

Budgeting isn't about restricting your spending; it's about expanding your options. It's about your quality of life. It's about peace, pleasure, and triumph. It's about feeling fulfilled, and creating big, beautiful memories—no matter how small your budget.

It's about being confident.

It's about being strong.

It's about being true to you.

And it's about loving yourself in ways you never have before.

CHAPTER TWO

Money Anxiety Isn't about Money

I was eleven years old the day my mom decided to divorce my father. I knew it was going to be bad.

Crash. Clang. Thud. Thwack.

My mom quickly grabbed a few belongings, including her favorite Japanese doll, and told us to get in the car. We rushed over to my grandma's house, where we barricaded ourselves in the bathroom—a measure that seemed necessary at the time. Huddled together in the shower, I watched my mother's face freeze, the phone held to her ear, as my father took an ax to all of the furniture in our house and threatened her life on the other end of the line.

Moments like these are the kinds that form the anxieties we'll face later in life, including financial anxiety. Perhaps you've been through something like what I have. Or perhaps you have lived or are living through true, severe scarcity, such as homelessness. No matter what type of trauma you've experienced—big, little, or something in between—that trauma unequivocally affects the way we view *everything*, especially the way we think about money. Because *how safe we feel* affects the way we think about money. Money anxiety doesn't arrive the minute we open our bank account or our credit cards; it's born during the times we've been made to feel scared.

For me, life after the divorce became a constant battle between money and us, as my mother worked three jobs to pay for activities for my sister and me. She went into debt just keeping the household afloat. We'd put all of our basic necessities, from school notebooks to underwear, on a credit card. Sometimes, she had no choice but to borrow money from my grandma to make ends meet. And of course, all of this anxiety trickled down into my own subconscious even further.

The trauma intensified.

While my mom is the strongest, kindest woman I know, she's also human: she's an emotional creature. And you are, too. Regardless of how strong you are, emotions always come into play. Fear and loneliness invade your psyche. You feel like you're waging the war alone. Nothing is easy, and everything feels up to chance. You're walking a constant tightrope, fighting for your happiness while forever worrying about not having enough.

It's exhausting. That exhaustion erodes your conviction. You start to *expect* life to be hard.

That's how I felt at the beginning of my financial journey, and it's how almost all of the women in my community have felt at some point. I call this kind of thinking a **scarcity mindset**, the persistent expectation that you will not have enough. And while that's a normal emotional response to trauma, it doesn't represent reality. While you may constantly feel like there's not enough money, that you're not good at getting money, that you're "bad at numbers," none of that is true.

It's your trauma talking.

True Story: From Trauma Filled to On Track

The Budget Mom Family member Ashley struggled with anxiety and scarcity thinking all her life. It worsened when she became a mom: she was tasked with worrying about not only herself but also the four little lives she was responsible for.

As a result, she also developed a new view on debt. When she had kids, it seemed essential to take out more personal loans, major credit cards, and store credit cards. Her rationale was no longer just "I'll save money this way because I get 20 percent off my first purchase" or "I could even pay more than the minimum payment if I wanted to!" but rather "What if my kids need something?"

Her mind raced with all of the bad things that could happen. She thought she knew the root of her issues, low self-esteem—about being overweight, a good mother, a good wife. Feeling constantly on the edge of a disaster, she began taking anxiety medications to calm her nerves. They made her feel tired and sluggish, but she told herself that if she just kept moving forward and taking it day by day, things would eventually get better.

But things did not get better. In order to cope with the anxiety, she turned to food. When she would leave for work or have a few moments in the car to herself, she'd sneak over to Dunkin' Donuts and buy an iced coffee and a donut. She told herself that she needed that coffee to get through the day, and the donut simply made her feel happier. On weekends, her kids would beg for a "special breakfast" from McDonald's. She felt like she couldn't say no, worried that depriving them of what they wanted would sour their image of her as a mom. This cycle of worrying, eating, and spending was exhausting her.

One day, she realized that her family was drowning in debt. The worst part was that she knew the things they had spent so much money on either ended up being donated, sold, or thrown away because they cluttered their home without bringing any real value. It became clear to her that she bought these "things" just to try to fill some void in her life. Her breaking point was an anxiety attack that felt more like a heart attack. Something had to change.

Like so many of us, Ashley once made all of her financial decisions in a state of panic. Driving her financial anxieties, of course, were more personal ones about her weight and about her ability as a mom. She found *The Budget Mom* with the simple intention of getting rid of debt, and by the end of the first month, she was doing great. For the first time ever, she actually had money left over after paying her bills. But then the panic set in: Should she really just give it away to a creditor?

She tried to think logically and rationally: "I'll be okay if I use this extra money toward this credit card, because if I pay down this credit card, I'll still have the equivalent available credit to use if I need something . . . BUT, what if the creditor then lowers my credit limit because I've now brought my balance down enough?!" This anxiety-fueled scarcity thinking almost prevented her from taking the first step toward a financially fulfilled life. It was blocking her view of the bigger picture.

Money Anxiety Isn't about Money

It was around this time that the trouble started with her husband. He's a combat veteran who suffers from PTSD and a traumatic brain injury, and he had developed a drinking problem to cope with some of his stressors. He was turning into someone she didn't recognize, and when he started to become verbally abusive, Ashley worried about keeping her kids in such a toxic environment. In her ten years of marriage, she couldn't have ever planned for this.

She started imagining all of the worst-case scenarios. At one point, she thought of leaving her husband and taking the kids. It was in that moment that reality hit her: her bad credit and lack of savings was holding her back from ever being able to act, were it necessary. She could never take control in the worst-case scenario. Her credit score was in the four hundreds, and she had no emergency fund set aside. Thankfully, she was able to get her husband help, but the thought lingered in her mind: she needed more financial stability.

After bingeing videos on my YouTube channel and mentally debating with herself, she finally decided to start building her emergency savings. Once that was fully funded, she decided to look into the Snowball Method. She took a deep breath and began to pay down credit cards, starting with the cards with the smallest balances.

Next, Ashley did something that reflected a true shift in her mindset: instead of making decisions based on a feeling of scarcity, she began to set boundaries with her money. She relied on her cash envelopes—more on that soon—and wrote down and highlighted all of her expenses on her expense tracker. Now, instead of charging every family outing to her credit card, she hides the cards away and limits her spending to the cash in her envelopes. She uses large bills so that "spending just a few dollars" isn't so easy. Tracking her spending is now effortless, because her bank account's focus is solely on bills and savings transfers.

In just a matter of months, Ashley regained control and, instead of finding herself drowning at the end of every month, consistently started having money left over after all of her bills were paid. Without any change in income, Ashley felt for the first time like she had enough. This is how the shift to an abundant mindset begins.

Notice how Ashley got there. She didn't start by asking herself, "Okay, how much money do I need?" and then counting an arbitrary number. She started by asking herself *what she wanted*. She wanted to make sure her children were never vulnerable, while living a more relaxed life. (Turns out, being in survival mode 24/7 is debilitating.)

Once Ashley changed her relationship with money, her mental health improved. And not only has her health improved, but she has since paid off not just one, but *three* credit cards. Her emergency savings are fully funded, and she's contributing to multiple sinking funds (more on those later, too!). Instead of worrying she won't have the security of the "extra money," she actually feels extreme relief. Slowly but surely, her credit is going up, and it's giving her a sense of self-worth that she hasn't felt for a very long time.

Ashley started her journey with the simple goal of paying off more debt, but along the way she found her purpose—her *why*. It's her emotional health so that she can be more present for herself and her family. Her worries have always stemmed from her finances, but they've disguised themselves under the stressors of everyday life. It's become abundantly clear to her that having a more secure financial future will provide her so much comfort mentally.

If she continues on this path, she anticipates that she will be free of credit card debt by the end of the year. Not only that, but she and her husband will also be able to take their kids on vacation for the first time in years, and she anticipates getting rid of at least one, if not all, of her medications. That sense of freedom—of life in abundance—makes her feel like a better mom than any Dunkin' Donuts donut ever has.

It's Not about the Numbers

More money isn't the solution; more strategy is. Consider that when Ashley first started making headway on her debt, she didn't earn a dollar more than when she started. That's proof that you don't need to win the lottery in order to finally get ahead: you can do it on your current income, no matter how hard things feel right now. (I promise.)

When people start budgeting for the first time, they do what most financial experts tell them to do and break out their calculators and start talking dollars and cents. They'll look at their debt and imagine how they can cut their expenses. They feel bad as they review their purchases. They wish they just had more income—and the shame spiral begins.

When I was starting my journey, I fell into this trap, too. I believed that more money—measured in numbers—was the solution. I used to tie my success to the numbers because I felt like numbers were the only "true, objective" way to see how much progress I was making. I set up huge (and, frankly, unrealistic) expectations of myself and was crushed when I didn't reach those goals. I compared my failures to other people's successes. I was miserable. I didn't have a strategy; all I had was a calculator. *And the two are not the same.*

But here's the thing: money does not make you wealthy. It doesn't matter how much money you make if you can't manage it well. You could make a million dollars today and spend $999,000 tonight. You could have hundreds of thousands of dollars saved, and then you could buy a house and an expensive car and then have nothing in your savings account.

You see my point? Having or making money means nothing if you can't manage your finances. I'll tell you now what I wish I knew back then: money alone doesn't equate to a happy or successful life. Managing the money you have to support a life you love—that's success. When you manage your money, you can use it to support what actually matters to you.

Looking back on the version of myself obsessed with numbers, I have a lot of compassion for her. She felt like she couldn't do anything right and constantly felt like she didn't have enough.

We're always told not to attach our emotions to money. We don't think about learning patience or kindness or joy. We automatically think, "I want to get better with my money. Let's start counting." And we compare ourselves to others, saying, "Well, this girl paid off $4,000 of debt in one month. Why can't I do that?"

But there are different questions we're not asking that could potentially help us far more:

What does success mean to her?

What is she working toward?

What does she have at her disposal (time, income)?

What responsibilities does she have (dependents, jobs)?

What processes work for her?

How does she do it?

Questions about priorities get at the life a person is trying to build, and it's a way more important question than "How much?"

I want people to celebrate the how: the wins of decreasing a grocery budget, of saving for holiday gifts, or anticipating a bill, or of adding to a bank account. When you manage your money well, your process will work no matter how much income you have.

It's a lie that numbers are all that matter. Because what I've found, time and time again, is that numbers are a misleading measure of financial confidence. Rather, you must put the numbers into perspective. In order to truly take back your financial life, you don't need to "make the numbers work"; you need to deal with the deeper question, the one I brought up earlier: What adds value to your life?

When we are too panicked to really go after what we want, of course we don't trust ourselves to make money decisions. We don't believe a life without worry is possible, so we fill our lives with whatever's handy: the nearest relationship, the next purchase, the next promotion. Whatever the distraction, it's keeping us from actually digging into our own needs, wants, and dreams. It's keeping us from envisioning and creating a life of abundance. We don't know ourselves well enough to really answer the question: What do I want?

Once you know what you truly want—what brings real value to your life—you will know how much is enough.

Finding Abundance

. . . .

The first step toward an abundant, happy life is accepting that a life without financial struggle is possible.

On this journey, you're going to need more than numbers to keep you motivated. What happens when you don't "hit the numbers" one month? If the numbers are all that matter to you, you might give up. If, however,

the *BUDGET BY PAYCHECK steps*

1. Determine your WHY and purpose
2. Track and categorize your spending
3. Identify regular bills
4. Cash envelopes and variable expenses
5. Budget calendar
6. Prioritize savings goals
7. Create a plan of attack for your debt
8. Create a realistic paycheck budget
9. Tweak and perfect for the future

what's important is your progress toward a healthier you and a life of value, then numbers—big or small—are not the point. The point is change, growth, action, and creating a life you love.

The advice in this book gets to the heart of a proven system, the Budget by Paycheck Method, that I have perfected over the years on my own financial journey, and which has helped women all around the world achieve their goals and find financial fulfillment.

By the time you're finished reading this book, you will:

1. discover your reason why—your ultimate purpose. You'll learn to use your own life and vision as motivation for your new financial practices.

2. build financial awareness and find out what feelings and beliefs are keeping you in destructive spending patterns.

3. prioritize your financial goals and learn how to prioritize according to your own life.

4. design a budget calendar and learn to budget according to your specific needs, income, and lifestyle.

5. create a realistic budget and learn how to avoid burnout.

6. build a connection to your spending and learn to separate needs from wants (and surprise yourself at how much you can save).

7. create a debt plan and find out what gives you energy to tackle your debt.

8. map a path to retirement and start treating retirement as more than a finish line.

9. invest for your goals and empower yourself to create your own future.

This plan will help you to build a strong emotional foundation and teach you the skills you need to chart your own path toward a life of abundance and financial fulfillment. It's not just about getting out of debt; it's about discovering why you're in debt in the first place (and what we're going to do about it). It's not just how to save, but what motivates the self-discipline you need to make saving money a priority in your life. It's not just what makes you happy in the moment, but how to use trade-offs to fund the life you want today and in the future.

It's not just about running the numbers; it's about living.

Part One

Build a New Foundation

CHAPTER THREE

Start by Answering This Question

Have you ever heard that you should check your emotions at the door when it comes to money? Emotions supposedly make you irrational and foolish, especially if you're a woman. And if you're married, a relationship counselor may have even told you not to bring up emotions when talking about money with your spouse to reduce the likelihood of conflict. The idea here is that leaving emotions out of the equation will lead you to make better, wiser, more objective financial decisions.

The Budget by Paycheck Method takes a different approach: emotions are a *part* of your money strategy.

The truth is, when it seems like "emotions are getting the best of us"—such as when I used to overspend out of guilt—we're actually suppressing them. Instead of investigating why I felt guilty, I simply tried to make the guilt go away. Instead of honoring that voice inside me that told me something wasn't right, I tried to shut it up by swiping my card.

What we don't realize is that the guilt I felt—or the panic that Ashley felt—are both signs of something deeper. I felt guilty because I *loved* my son, and I wanted to make the best life I could for him. Once I focused on that love instead of my guilt, I was able to harness my emotions toward positive spending patterns. It wasn't logic but emotion that powered me through the burnout, the setbacks, and the mistakes I made over the years on this journey to pay off my debt. Turns out, logic can only get you so far.

You don't have to have a life-altering event, like having a baby, to motivate your financial journey. But you *do* need to start asking yourself questions you haven't asked before. You need to uncover your real priorities in life. And you need to lean on your emotions as a guide. Because emotion is the only thing that gives you true conviction when things get hard. Make no mistake, you *will* screw up. You'll have rough days. You'll fail with your budget, you'll spend money when you shouldn't, and there are going to be days where you ask yourself, "Why am I even doing this?"

Your job is to make sure you know the answer. Here we need to add that the most important thing is to make sure that your emotions are not controlling your decisions. Instead, you want to be making financial decisions based on clearly understanding your emotions and being able to control them.

Not a surface-level answer, but the deeper motivations that are driving your spending—both positively and negatively. It's not about just being debt-free; it's about what being debt-free means to you. Nor is it just about owning a home; it's the experiences and memories you'll make in that home. And, of course, it's not just about saving money; it's about the freedom to have choices and the financial stability that gives you peace of mind. When you connect your financial journey with those parts of your life, you'll experience more drive and discipline than you ever have before. What you're fighting for is a life that's better than the one you have today. I can personally attest to that, and so can hundreds of thousands of The Budget Mom Family members who have put these principles into practice for themselves. There's a richer, freer, fuller life in front of you than anything you are about to leave behind.

Uncovering Your Deep Motivation: How to Find Your *Why*

TBM Family member Jeanine learned from a young age that money simply wasn't something she had—and she never questioned that. Growing up, she sensed that her parents didn't have a lot of it; why else would they take the kids to McDonald's and not order anything for themselves?

Jeanine ended up becoming a hard, diligent worker, but she struggled to feel confident in her own skin. Most of the $25K she made per year working as a server went to massages and makeup to compensate for a lack of self-esteem. She couldn't manage to save up for much-needed dental work or other basic needs. While she inherited the mindset that money is taboo, sometimes there was just no escaping reality: it often hit her on her walk to work that if she didn't make enough in tips, the lights would be turned off by the time she got home from her shift.

Her low self-esteem didn't just affect her financial health; it affected all the decisions she made. She dated people she knew she shouldn't, and at the end of one particularly bad relationship, found herself evicted from her apartment and crippled by insurmountable debt. Once her debt went into collections, she struggled even more to stay afloat. When her car was repossessed, she knew something had to change.

Jeanine found the Budget Mom Community in 2019 and immediately began applying the principles you'll learn in this book. She embraced the cash envelope system we'll visit soon and began saving more money than she ever had. Then she got a new job that almost doubled her restaurant salary, and even developed a relationship with a new partner who helped her believe she could reach her financial goals. And yet, she still wasn't making a dent in her actual debt. Why did it feel like everyone in the community was making progress besides her?

When she took a hard look at her spending tracker and saving funds, it immediately became obvious why she was spinning her wheels: Jeanine was spending money on everyone but herself. She would delay putting money toward her debts in order to stuff her cash envelopes for dates and dinners and gifts and other things she knew would bring her partner joy. She was compensating for her low self-esteem by spending on others. Realizing that she needed to put herself first—which included putting her debt first—she paused her relationship to get her priorities straight.

She began earning extra money through gig work and put all her earnings toward her debt. She created new sinking funds that would specifically add value to *her* life: moving to be closer to her sick father, budgeting for a vacation with friends, spending money on improving her home, and setting aside six months of emergency savings for peace of mind. She dyed her hair pink and got her nose pierced, expressing herself more authentically for the first time in years. And she took up the practice of gratitude journaling only to realize that she not only loved herself, but—to her surprise—she also really loved this thing she once feared. She *loved* money. She loved managing it, budgeting it, saving it, and spending it well, with purpose and intention, as she had learned how to do. It changed her life—so much so that she then offered to help her ex with his company's finances. Her efforts were a success, and soon she didn't just have a job, she had an all-new passion. She kept going, kept offering to help, kept working with money, and today, Jeanine makes her living helping all types of companies with their finances.

What a transformation.

Jeanine's motivation ended up being *her own personal development.* She wanted to grow herself and grow her career, and maybe that's true for you, too. You are allowed to be motivated by your own self-interest. Whether it's finding a career that fills you with joy, improving your self-image, or living a purpose-driven life, it's okay if your *why* isn't to foster world peace. But you still need to know what your goals are so we know how to direct your finances.

So go ahead and humor me: grab a notebook and a pen, or, if you're listening, simply close your eyes, and think about your purpose. To help guide you, I'm going to suggest the steps that I have seen help a broad, diverse range of women begin to define theirs.

Step 1: Start with a Goal, Then Ask the Next Question

For example, maybe your goal is paying off your debt. But then ask the next question: *"So what?"* Why do you want to pay off debt? What emotions come up for you around paying off debt? Do you feel it will give you more opportunities? Do you feel it will improve your lifestyle? Do you feel like it will make you a happier person? Is it to live the fullest life possible with your family without relying on someone else's money? What is the reason behind the goal? Or, even better, what's the reason behind the reason?

Let's say your goal is freedom. *So what?* What does freedom mean to you? Does it mean that you can do things with your children without worrying about your checking account balance? Does it mean being able to travel without going into debt to achieve it? Does it mean that you can stop living paycheck to paycheck and start building wealth for your family?

I had one client tell me, "My *why* is to have financial stability." She was a single woman without kids, who had accrued debt through credit card spending and by taking out a car loan.

I asked her the next question: "*So what?* Why do you want to have financial stability? What does that mean to you?"

That simple question opened up a floodgate. She said, "Because I don't want to feel stressed out every time something goes wrong. I don't constantly want to be in panic mode. I don't want to feel like I'm always struggling."

It was clear to me: her deeper *why* was to bring peace to her life.

Step 2: Make a Goal Bigger than Yourself

Ask yourself, "Who or what in my life do my finances affect besides me?"

It's a clarifying question. Say you want to pay off debt, and you want to pay off that debt because you want more freedom in your life to do what you love. How would you having more freedom affect the people around you?

Before I had my son, I didn't really know what I wanted to do in my future. I got up and went to work. I didn't feel like I had much purpose.

My son gave me a deep sense of purpose. Raising him gives me the feeling of being part of something bigger than myself for the first time.

So who or what else do your finances affect? It doesn't have to be a child; another member of the Budget Mom Family keeps her pets in mind as she budgets! Another member mentions her parents, hoping to pay off their debts so they don't have to. Whatever it is, it's helpful when your *why* goes beyond just you. This deeper, broader sense of purpose is essential for a lasting *why*.

Step 3: Attach a Visual

When I dreamed about buying a house in cash, I could literally see my son running through the front door playing with our dog. I could hear his laughter. I could see us on the porch swing as the sun set. I could feel it. That image is what motivated me to save—and to resist the temptation to spend.

People tell me, "Miko, I want a life without debt." That's a great start, but it doesn't go far enough. It has no *image* connected to it. I want you to be able to envision and visualize your life without debt: when you say it out loud, you need to be able to see it in your future and hear it in your mind and actually feel what that reality would be like.

When I think about my *why*, I think about my son, who is a competitive wrestler, traveling for weekend competitions. I imagine him making friends with the other participants. I imagine him giving it his all on the mat. I also imagine him going to college one day, whatever college he wants to go to. I imagine him with textbooks under his arm, and excelling in a subject that he loves, or discovering a passion. I imagine him sitting in a classroom and raising his hand. Most of all, I imagine us spending time together in our own home, watching a movie on our couch, playing with our dog, or eating breakfast at the kitchen table.

Once you get to that place where you can visualize your goal—when you can feel it and see what you're fighting for—it becomes far more powerful than "being debt-free."

Discipline versus Motivation

Motivation is a key part of your financial journey, but it's not enough on its own. Motivation is the kick-starter, but it can never guarantee success. If you want a true, long-lasting financial transformation, you have to discover and practice discipline.

There will be times when motivation is lost. Motivation, by its nature, comes and goes. When it hits, you can harness an unusual sense of power and productivity. But this unstoppable feeling is unreliable and you can't control it.

But you can *choose* discipline.

I like to think of motivation as a separate being from myself who chooses when to come around. I can't beg, force, or manipulate motivation into sticking around longer than it wants to.

So how do you find this everlasting desire to continue on your financial transformation, even when you don't feel motivated? It takes consistent self-discipline in your daily life.

If motivation is the "why" on your journey, discipline is your "what." Self-discipline is simply correcting or regulating your financial behavior for the sake of improvement. It is the deliberate practice of sitting down with your budget planner every Monday and updating your spending, even if you don't feel like confronting your account balance after a weekend vacation. It is the unwavering adherence to your financial boundaries, such as steering clear of the mall on a Saturday afternoon even if stress or boredom calls. Discipline is the best tool you have to help you get back on the right track when you fall off your path.

Motivation and discipline go hand in hand. Motivation can be your initial inspiration. When you lose your inspiration, self-discipline steps in and will keep you going.

Marks of a Lasting *Why*

You may already have an idea of your *why*. Or maybe it's not immediately obvious and you're feeling stuck. Either way, I want to walk you through the following criteria for coming up with a motivating, lasting *why*.

1. A *Why* Evokes Emotion

Take a minute and think about the last time you got emotional. Like, *really* emotional. Maybe you cried at a scene in a movie or fired off a furious email. Maybe you felt afraid of losing a friend or family member—or maybe you did actually have to say goodbye. Whatever comes to mind first, go with that. Take a minute and put yourself back in that moment. Breathe deeply and remember what it felt like to be there.

That level of emotion has to be present in your motivation.

That's why your *why* has to make you *feel* something. This is a requirement. Your *why* should be something so important that you get emotional just talking about it.

Feelings keep us motivated. So many TBM community members'

stories inspire me. One TBM community member shared how her *why* comes from her experience of being too dependent on her partner. After their difficult split, she realized the importance of self-reliance and owning her own home. When she shared this with our online community, I could hear the emotion right through the screen.

2. A *Why* Is Specific

Even when you get to your *why*, don't stop there. Make it as specific as possible.

For example, you already know that my son is my ultimate *why*. But just saying that—"my son is my *why*"—doesn't actually help me visualize the future I want to have. Over time, I've learned to communicate my vision in more specific, concrete terms. Now my *why* reads: "Living a life with my son where I can seize opportunities with him without relying on debt." My *why* is my quality of life that I live with him and the ability to do that on my own terms in my own way. That's a specific *why*. It is big enough to cover many areas (buying a home in cash or helping him pay for his education, for example) but specific enough to help me prioritize my goals and filter my money decisions.

Your *why* is unique to you: it could have to do with your family, your history, or your personal goals. When reaching for a specific *why*, ask yourself, "What's important to me about this *why?*" One TBM community member gave a great example when she said that it wasn't just her children that motivated her but teaching her children new spending and saving patterns. Like so many, she wanted the generational struggle to end with her.

3. A *Why* Is Something You Can't Imagine Going Without

Whenever I need a boost of motivation, I ask myself, "What happens if I fail? What do our lives look like if I give up?" Any time I feel like giving up, I look at my son's face. When I do that, I remember that giving up is not an option, because I would be giving up on *him*.

Think about the consequences of giving up on your *why*. If it's important enough to you, giving up will not be an option.

What to Avoid When Finding Your *Why*

. . . .

I once had a client who was struggling with her *why*. She was newly single, had just been through a divorce, didn't have kids, and was ready to focus on herself and her career. She told me, "So many people say that they want to be financially stable for their families. But I don't have a family and I'm not sure if I even want one. What could my *why* possibly be?"

Your *why* might be a person—people often choose partners or family members. But maybe for you it's not a person at all. After a deep discussion, I helped my client uncover a different *why*: She wanted to travel. She wanted to be able to afford one beautiful, big trip per year.

On the other hand, others make it too simple. They don't dig far enough with their *why*. They make it about debt payoff or savings or a balanced budget. None of that is visual or emotional. That's the means to the end, not the end itself.

If your *why* changes over time, that's okay! If it's something with a specific date—like a trip or a specified savings goal—then you can just reassess once the date passes.

But that first *why* might also be a clue to a deeper *why*.

For example, if you want to take your mom to New York City before her fiftieth birthday, that's a onetime event. But that *why* shows us that your mom is important to you. That trip may pass, but perhaps it leads you to a bigger goal: it might be that you want to retire early so you can spend as much time as possible with your mom. That's a *why* rooted in emotion.

There's a reason why you want to be successful with your money. There's a reason why you picked up this book. Even if your *why* came to you right away, I encourage you to spend some time reflecting on *why* that's your *why*. Really think about it and reflect. You might say "my kids," and that's a great start. But what is it about your children that makes you want to get better with your finances? Is it that you want to send them to college? Do you want to be able to take them on family vacations? Do you want them to learn positive money habits from you? Try to examine your underlying motivations.

Sometimes, when I ask people what their *why* is, they say, "I want to buy a car," or, "I want to pay off debt," or, "I want to save more money." The sentence starts with "I," and it's all about "I"—and that's the first clue that you might be able to go deeper. Once you make your journey about something more than yourself, you'll discover the source of your true motivation.

What You Miss When You Skip the *Why*

A financially fulfilled life will mean different things to different people, which is why it's so important to understand what it means to you. Doing the work to uncover your *why* and to visualize the way I've shown you in this chapter will mean the difference between success and failure when it comes to money.

So many people skip this step. They don't take time to really reflect on their *why* or deeper motivation. They jump right into tactics and spreadsheets. And unfortunately, that's the fastest way to fail at money: not understanding what you want it *for*.

When you discover your *why*, you discover your purpose. You're embarking on a mission and drawing a map for your money. You aren't just sitting there, letting life happen to you. You're taking inventory of what you've got, what you want, and how you're going to make it happen.

And you won't just become financially successful.

You're going to be successful, period.

Make It Happen

Make a list of all your possible *whys*.

Ask yourself, "What gets me up in the morning?"

Ask yourself, "What can't I live without?"

Write every answer you can think of.

Make It Visual

Get specific here. For each possible *why*, answer:

What will your life be like?

Who will be around you?

What kinds of activities will you do?

What physical things are around you?

Find a photo or another visual reminder to put up in your house, keep in your wallet, or place at your desk to remind you of your *why*.

Make It Emotional

How does each *why* make you feel?

Circle three that really stand out to you.

Make yourself a reminder.

For Those Following along with the Budget by Paycheck Method

Go to Step #1: Figure out your *why* in your *Budget by Paycheck® Workbook*.

CHAPTER FOUR

The Real Reason You Buy (Hint: You Don't Like H&M *That* Much)

My spending habits (and spending problems) developed early in life, starting with the first time I saw the movie *Working Girl*. If you don't know *Working Girl*, we'll remedy that right after we remedy your finances. It's a must-see classic with Melanie Griffith, who plays a secretary working her way up the corporate ladder by breaking all the rules. She pretends to be someone she isn't—her boss—and changes her appearance, starts wearing gorgeous shoes and clothes, mimics her boss's every move, and eventually ends up with a huge promotion at work (not to mention the guy).

As a little girl, I *loved* this movie. And through it, I developed this image of the type of woman I wanted to become: what I wanted to look like, act like, be like. By the time I got to college, I had developed this craving for fashion and clothes, the material things that I subconsciously believed would open the gates to my own future.

But as you might imagine, with all the new clothes came the expensive hair, nail, and waxing appointments, new shoes, tanning sessions, and more. Eventually I racked up seven credit cards—*seven*—and tons of student loan debt, and I had absolutely zero plans to turn my spending around: I hadn't yet reached the Melanie Griffith version of myself.

Behind all my overspending was a young woman wrestling with self-confidence, uncomfortable in her own skin. I struggled with my appearance. I didn't feel like I fit in. I wasn't sure who I was or what I wanted. Whenever I was feeling sad or depressed, I would go to the mall and buy clothes. I would feel good about myself for a short time, but before I knew it, I'd need another hit of dopamine as I found myself scouring the racks, once again, spending money on ridiculous things I didn't need in order to find happiness from things that never made me happy in the past. And when I'd finally maxed out my credit cards, I made yet another stunning decision:

I applied for more financial aid.

I didn't see that my desire to be "perfect" was fueling my spending. All I saw was a bag that I needed or shoes that would complete the look. And when I dared to glance at my bank statements, all that registered was a big *F* for failure. I didn't stop to think, "Maybe something deeper is going on here."

A Life without Awareness: Spending Money in the Dark

Spending became a habit and a reward—even something to do when I was bored or needed a break from the chaos of home. Later, as a young professional, I would go to the mall after a hectic workday just to get a moment to myself before going home to my son. I'd think to myself, "I'll just walk around." Pretty soon, I was popping in to "browse" the sales racks at H&M, as usual.

Speaking of H&M, one day I was there with maybe $400 in my checking account and hardly enough money to cover the bills, but that didn't affect my shopping! (That's what my *new* credit card was for.) My pile of clothes was up to my chin with everything I was going to buy: skirts, blouses, belts, rhinestone-covered hair accessories. If they sold it, I wanted it. *This was my drug.*

As I stood there in the checkout line that day, I heard the girl behind me talking to her mom. Overhearing their conversation, I instantly went numb.

She was asking for her mother's credit card.

And suddenly, I saw a glimpse of my own future: I might be dependent on this piece of plastic for life. I might forever be trapped by a cheap, twelve-dollar H&M T-shirt. I looked down at the things I had in my arms and removed myself from the line.

This experience is what I call a slap-in-the-face moment. It's a moment when we have the courage to look at our situation truthfully, at our real spending habits. At the real emotions behind those spending habits. It can be painful. It can be devastating. And if you're anything like me, it will bring up massive feelings of guilt. And that's why I avoided being honest about my spending for a long, long time: I was scared to know the truth about myself. It was so easy for me to swipe my credit card (and feel the guilt later), rather than face the truth in the present. I avoided looking at bank statements closely. I shut my eyes when my credit card statements came. I didn't want to count the number of items— or see the dollar amount—of what I was spending at the mall or the salon. They weren't just numbers and line items; they were tiny little reminders of my own flaws.

I was keeping myself in the dark on purpose; I didn't want that kind of proof. I couldn't see my own situation for what it was; therefore, making progress was impossible. Not only was I completely unaware of how much money I was spending on clothes and beauty appointments per month, but I was also avoiding the reason I was spending so much in the first place.

Unresolved emotional conflict.

With money, there's *always* something deeper going on, and spending is always connected to your emotions. Finances are emotional! When you finally have your slap-in-the-face moment, you might see some big numbers that you owe: those numbers are telling the story of something internal. The first step to winning your battle with money is looking in the mirror and facing reality head-on.

How much are you spending? What are you spending it on? If you feel like your spending is out of control—or if you feel like no matter what financial goals you set for yourself, you keep finding yourself in the same place—you're likely also battling a source of unresolved emotional conflict.

And that means your emotional problems are ruling your wallet.

For me, chasing this posh "image" of myself was costing me quite a lot. I wasn't buying clothes because I truly liked the items; I was buying the clothes because *I didn't like myself.*

Today I refer to this as developing **decision-making awareness**: an understanding of why you act as you do and what needs to change. It's the ability to identify patterns, establish the reason behind the patterns, and adjust based on that. I became aware of why I was spending, which allowed me to stop spending on clothes and start addressing the real issue inside.

For example, maybe a large portion of your income goes toward eating out. You might tell yourself that you eat out for convenience—who wants to make dinner after a long day at work? However, perhaps the deeper reason you overspend on eating out is that you're stressed at work. That makes you feel frantic, like you never have any time for yourself. As a result, you find yourself in a pattern of dining out at expensive restaurants as a way of subconsciously "getting revenge." Finally, something for *you.* After all, you deserve it, right? But what you're really doing is using money to lick your emotional wounds. And that's precisely what you need to address *first* if you want to get your finances in check; it's not about the restaurants, it's about the stress. Figure out why you feel stressed all the time and your overspending will begin to heal.

That's decision-making awareness. And the best way to build it is to be completely and unabashedly honest with yourself. For example, once I began tracking all of my expenses on a physical piece of paper and highlighting every category in different colors, I was forced to confront my habits head-on.

But when you live in the dark about where you are financially, you'll repeatedly find yourself stuck in the same spending patterns. You'll feel a resistance to looking up your total debt or reviewing your bank statements. You'll make goals and priorities but not be able to deliver on them. You'll go to the store and just "have" to buy "it," whatever "it" is.

You can't control your finances until you bring awareness into your financial life. Face your situation, then reflect on what the underlying issues are that are causing that situation.

What Kind of Spender Are You?

Like many members of the TBM Family, Cassie grew up with very little financial education and very little cash. She watched her mother get by on next to nothing, barely being able to cover groceries with an "allowance" from her stepfather. Cassie wasn't sure how to help her mom, but she knew that any time she was successful—at anything, really—it made her mother happy. And since Cassie naturally wanted to continue being "a good girl," she went to great lengths to continue to be "successful"—at least, what she thought it meant then.

Therefore, when Cassie was accepted into the University of California, she readily took on all the loans made available to her: this was her ticket to a better life. And when Cassie had the opportunity to open a credit card with a higher credit limit, she took it. (She hoped that zero percent APR meant that she didn't have to pay balances each month—not at all what that means.)

Shortly after she graduated, she began receiving letters requiring her to pay off the loans. She struggled to make the minimum payments on both of her credit cards. She even tried to open a third credit card but was denied. But when she was accepted into a master's program, her loans were deferred. She felt incredibly relieved, saved from her crushing monthly payments. But of course the peace was short-lived.

Her slap-in-the-face moment came in 2018. She was sitting in the passenger seat of her boyfriend's car in an Albertson's parking lot, crying. There, she confessed that she was unable to pay her half of their rent. She was mortified.

That night she spent hours reviewing her spending habits. Looking at her bank and credit card statements, she realized she spent much of her income on items like clothing subscription boxes, Amazon purchases, and whatever made her feel happy at the time. She couldn't imagine how, on a $52,000 salary (successful!), she was struggling. But after reviewing her actual spending patterns, Cassie realized that her salary wasn't enough to pay all of the debt she'd accumulated. How would she ever pay off her credit card ($7,000 with 24.99 percent APR) and student loans (over $160,000), and still manage to make her monthly bills?

On top of it all, she was also helping her mom financially; while she was happy to do this, it wasn't something she had planned. (Like me, she was also a big fan of the "winging it" method.) While her boyfriend graciously covered the rent that month, she felt ashamed enough to throw herself into budgeting.

That's when she found *The Budget Mom* and realized, as she examined her deeper motives, that much of her spending centered on her dynamic with her mother. She had always wanted her mother to be proud of her, and that was causing her to make irresponsible financial decisions in order to "play the part." Cassie realized that a large part of her unhappiness was all about maintaining this facade—not just with her mother, but with any adults who might be judging her success, including her mother's inner circle of friends. In other words, her entire life was about pleasing people with whom she hardly had *a relationship*. With that

43

realization, her *why* quickly changed from wanting to impress others to wanting financial independence.

But getting there would be tough.

When she began her journey out of debt, Cassie's budget reflected her embarrassment: she punished herself for the situation she had gotten herself into. She refused to spend money on any fun activities with friends or family or any type of self-care. Beyond feeling stressed about her strict budget, she felt conflicted about where to spend the money she did earn. As she graduated and received a pay raise, she looked to others to know what to do: she typed into her internet browser "Should I be putting money into a savings account?" and "I don't have a 401(k) . . . should I open up a Roth IRA?" She felt overwhelmed and unbearably confused.

However, after finding *The Budget Mom*, she heard me talk about the radical goal of *enjoying* the journey of getting out of debt—that the most successful budgeters are *not* the strictest (you don't have to be), and that you're allowed to enjoy yourself along the way. (In fact, pleasure is a requirement of my method.)

Soon, she learned my Budget by Paycheck system and began to budget her income and expenses in a whole new way—which, yes, included learning how to create a much-needed "fun" envelope for herself.

One year later, Cassie's situation has dramatically changed. She paid off over $15,000 of her student loans. She added money into her savings account for an emergency fund—plenty to give her peace of mind. She opened a Roth IRA and created a sinking fund for her mom. (This way, she could help in a responsible way when needed.) She also created additional sinking funds for holidays, medical expenses, and car expenses alike. She stopped relying on credit cards and began to make purchases with cash or with her debit card. And she started focusing on spending with intention—and purchasing the things she *did* want in her life—

instead of restricting her spending to only accommodate the random chaos of things she didn't.

The end result? A confident, relaxed, capable, financially successful Cassie. Even though she's still paying off debt and working toward her goals, she finally feels at ease in her life. She has the confidence she needs not to have to panic about her remaining debt because she's got a plan for it: She knows where her money is going and how long it will take to pay off. She knows what it's like to feel stable. She knows that one emergency or unexpected expense won't set her on course for disaster.

In other words, she's what I call **financially fulfilled**. It's the pride she feels as she asks a financial advisor important questions regarding Roth IRAs (questions that she would never have known to ask a year ago). It's the big smile on *my* face when she highlights another debt as paid off. It's the bear hugs from Jake, her boyfriend, for achieving her goals—and not just because he doesn't have to pay all the rent! It's the ability to work with her mom on *her* financial stability. It's her confidence to have financial conversations without crying about her situation. It's her sense of security, knowing that she is slowly building funds for her future children and her retirement. It's having the courage to make small changes, trusting that they'll have a big impact.

Because they do. They really, really do.

Before she found The Budget Mom Family, Cassie was what I call a **compulsive buyer**. For her, buying things was a way to address a problem that could not actually be fixed with money: her self-esteem.

The root cause needs to be identified—even though, if you're like most of us, you'd rather not know the truth of what you're actually spending on food delivery, at the mall, or online. Depending on your situation, this confrontation with your real spending habits can be shocking, and frankly scary. I get it, and as you know, I've been there.

However, a simple way to start this conversation is to ask yourself, without looking at any monthly totals, whether you can guess how much you spend each month. The actual number is going to be higher than you realize—it almost always is—but you'll never know until you take that first step.

And second, decide which one of the following types of spenders you think you are. Which resonates with you the most?

The Recycle Spender: This person makes purchases only to feel guilty about the money and return the same items. This becomes a cycle: buy, return, buy, return. This cycle runs on guilt. If you identify with this one, ask yourself what the source of your guilt might be. Do you feel guilty about your debt, or how it affects your family?

The Hoarder: The hoarder collects their money and does not spend or invest it. They often pay for things, even big purchases, in cash.

The Compulsive Buyer: This person buys to address a need or problem. Often the problem has to do with themselves, problems that cannot actually be fixed with money, like self-esteem.

The Impulsive Spender: This person spends on a whim. When they see something they want, they put their card down.

The FOMO Spender: These shoppers go to thrift stores and shop sales. To them, the cheapest price is the best. They are always afraid of missing out on a deal.

The Magnify Shopper: This person spends to celebrate, to make a moment special or memorable. They want to make a feeling bigger (magnify it) by making a purchase.

The Bored Buyer: This person shops because they need a distraction or something to keep them entertained.

This isn't even an exhaustive list. The full list could go on for pages. But chances are good you'll see yourself in one or more of these types of spenders—and that's perfectly normal. I remember a time when I was between relationships, I was both a compulsive buyer and a bored buyer. I'd go to the mall because I felt lonely and needed to be around people, and then I'd make purchases to make myself feel better.

What these types of spenders have in common is that they are *emotional* spenders. We all are. No matter how logical you are in other areas of your life, *money is always tied to emotion.* You can't stop emotional spending but you can control it. And that's what we're going to talk about next.

CHAPTER FIVE

The $1,000 Manicure—and Highlighting Your Blind Spots

To get at the deeper issues behind spending, I teach people how to examine their relationship with money.

Perhaps you've never thought of yourself as having a relationship with your money, but you're absolutely in one. And, just like other relationships, it can be healthy or it can be toxic.

Your relationship with money is very complex; many things influence the dynamic, but there are *two* major factors that really shape how we acquire, spend, and manage our money.

The first (and often most significant) factor: the messages you picked up as a child about the value of money. Starting at a very young age, we're bombarded with all kinds of subconscious messages about money, and those subconscious messages stay with us throughout our lifetime. What your parents or caretakers modeled for you about money created a framework in your mind; it taught you how to feel about money and how to use it. For example, if your parents didn't spend a lot of money, always preferring thrift stores and deal shopping, you learned that you can only spend money when there's a sale. On the other hand, maybe your parents spent plenty of money but went deep into debt to do so: they often spent money on dinner out, clothes, and vacations. Therefore, you learned that it's okay to go into debt; what's most important is having a good time now. How your caretakers treated money influenced the way that you will someday treat money, and sometimes it requires a bit of mental rewiring.

The second factor that massively influences the way you view money is the types of experiences you've had over the course of your lifetime. As you began to manage your own money, maybe you struggled to make ends meet. Maybe you had an unplanned emergency and had to spend a lot of money at once. (Those kinds of experiences might make you a more cautious spender.) Alternatively, maybe you never questioned your cash flow because a parent or spouse supported you wholly, or maybe your parents never brought you into financial discussions at all. (These types of situations might make you a thoughtless spender, someone who spends money without considering the consequences.)

The financial narrative you developed early on in life is susceptible to change, thanks to a wide variety of circumstances that are constantly altering your perception of money and your relationship to it. Significant life changes, in particular, have a massive impact on the relationship we adopt. For example, if you get super sick or have a near-death experience, you might abandon your previous thrifty mentality and, instead, go in the opposite direction and spend loads on experiences to make the most of the life you have.

This is why all money relationships are unique; they're each extremely personal. Even siblings raised in the same household grow up having very different relationships with money, because all of us process and organize the money messages we received as children in very different ways. Sometimes we mimic what our parents did, spending as they would have; other times we rebel and do the exact opposite.

Dr. Eileen F. Gallo-Ross, a psychotherapist who specializes in the emotional issues of family wealth, often speaks about what she calls the three dimensions of money: acquiring it, spending it, and managing it. Within each dimension you'll find yourself somewhere along a spectrum, according to your money beliefs.

The first dimension is acquisition. How do you bring money into your life? How much money do you need in order to feel secure?

You'll quickly see how your personal experiences and beliefs influence this dimension of spending. Maybe you believe that money is the root of all evil; you might not spend that much time devoted to acquiring it. Or on the other end of the spectrum, perhaps you believe that you can never have enough money; you might spend all your time devoted to this pursuit.

One end of the dimension of acquisition is apathy around earning money—total avoidance of it. On the other end is the constant pursuit of money—total insatiability. Where do *you* fall? How much time and energy (mental, emotional, and physical energy) do you spend trying to gain more money?

The second dimension is spending. Once you acquire money, a new question arises: What will you do with that money? Maybe you know someone who is a penny-pincher their entire life and ends up leaving this world with a considerable sum in their bank accounts. You may also hear about people who make millions of dollars but end up with nothing. On one side of the spectrum are people who hoard wealth, and on the other side are people who spend compulsively.

Where do you fall on *this* spectrum? Do you keep the money you have or spend it without thinking?

The third dimension is management. On one side is a person who tracks every cent; they're hyper-organized and controlling with their money. On the other end, however, you have a person who is completely disorganized and is unaware of the condition of their finances.

Where do you fall here? Are you controlling and obsessive, or are you disorganized and slapdash?

Ahealthy relationship with money requires balance in each of the three dimensions. Your acquisition, your spending, and your management of money need to create a life of contentment and peace.

So let's take a look at your relationship with money right now. Ask yourself these questions:

How do you feel about money?

What's happening in the world of your finances in your personal life?

What are your spending triggers? (In what situations do you find yourself itching to spend money?)

Can you identify where you are on these spectrums (acquisition, spending, management) right now?

How to Bring Awareness to Your Spending

Step 1: Track Your Spending

The first step to bringing awareness into your financial life is to see where your money is currently going. The best way to see where your money goes is to track your spending. (It isn't as painful as it sounds; you'll actually end up feeling quite proud!)

tbm MARCH Expense Tracker STARTING BALANCE: $1,087.26

CHECKING

Date	Account	Transaction	Category	Withdrawal	Deposit	Ending Balance
3/2	Income	TBM Pay	Income		4232 00	3328.76
3/2	Income	Chris Inc.	Income		600 00	5519.26
3/2	STCU	Car Maint	Savings	40 00		5479.26
3/2	STCU	Vacation	Savings	100 00		5379.26
3/2	STCU	Daycare	James	100 00		5279.26
3/2	STCU	Envelopes	Envelopes	1250 00		4023.26
3/3	STCU	Disneyland	Savings	269 00		3754.26
3/4	STCU	HughesNet	Income		89 98	3844.24
3/5	STCU	Rent	Home	850 00		
3/6	STCU	AT&T	Utilities	107 14		2827.10
3/6	STCU	Spotify	Utilities	10 88		2816.22
3/7	STCU	Hulu	Utilities	13 05		2803.17
3/10	STCU	Garbage	Utilities	73 88		2729.29
3/11	STCU	Internet	Utilities	114 26		2615.03
3/12	STCU	FE Savings	Savings	100 00		2515.03
3/16	STCU	Dental Ins	Insurance	21 79		2493.24
3/16	STCU	Avista	Utilities	348 50		2144.74
3/17	STCU	Checks	Misc	25 39		2119.35
3/17	STCU	529 Savings	Savings	450 00		1669.35
		County	Home	53 32		
3/20	STCU	Car Wash	Car	21 75		1594.28
3/20	STCU	Amazon	Beauty	13 67		1580.61
3/21	STCU	Gas	Gas	28 82		1551.79
3/22	STCU	Albertsons	Food	12 84		1538.95
3/22	STCU	Amazon	Cat	30 80		1508.15
3/23	STCU	Netflix	Utilities	14 15		1494.00
3/25	STCU	Life Ins.	Insurance	8 10		1485.90
3/25	STCU	Car Ins.	Insurance	116 75		1369.15
3/25	STCU	Pet Ins.	Pet	90 43		1278.72

Gather up all of your receipts and bank statements from the last month. Then, make a list. I use The Budget Mom monthly expense tracker, but even just a sheet of paper will do. On the left-hand side, write each amount of money you spent, and on the right-hand side go ahead and identify each expense. Don't forget to write out all of your spending: credit, debit, *and* cash (an easy one to forget!).

It's best if you can track a couple of months' worth of expenses. Again, don't forget to include credit card and cash spending. Then, I want you to examine your spending as a whole. You're looking for patterns. What consistency do you see, week to week or month to month? Write down your observations.

If tracking everything you spent last month seems impossible, that's okay. You can track this month. Going forward, write down every time you pay for something or swipe a card. Also, be sure to list automatic payments: any kind of subscription or automatic bill payment. In other words, every time money leaves your account or you use your credit card, write it down. If you are spending cash, saving your receipts will help. Save your receipts throughout the day and track your spending in the evening.

This is kind of like keeping a food journal when you're trying to identify a food allergy or other health condition. It can feel a little overwhelming to write down everything you eat (you eat as many as a dozen times during the day!), but sometimes seeing it on paper is the only way to fully grasp what's happening.

Step 2: Create Budget Categories

Tracking your spending lays it all out for you to see; the next step is to organize it. First, determine your budget categories. Budget categories are groups of expenses. Some of your budget categories might be:

Household expenses

Groceries

Transportation

School expenses

Clothes

These are just a few; chances are good you'll have many, and some of your categories will be unique to you.

To help me identify budget categories, I break out the highlighters. I'm a visual learner, so I get motivated in my budgeting when I see it laid out clearly and colorfully. As I look over my purchases, I start grouping them by color. For example, all gas transactions are highlighted yellow, all clothing purchases are highlighted in blue, all coffee transactions are highlighted in green, all makeup purchases are highlighted with pink. Once all transactions are highlighted in different colors, I add up all the pink transactions, all of the blue transactions, etc. Then, once all transactions are highlighted, I total them up to see how much I'm spending in each category. I call this **the highlighter method.**

People often ask me how many categories—and how many highlighter colors—they need. Should I have five, twenty, or one hundred? There isn't a "right" number of categories, but you will know how many you need, the more you do it. For example, when you don't have enough categories, it's hard to know what you're actually spending money on— so you won't get the clarity you need. If I used a budget category called "family" to budget for my son's clothes, his wrestling lessons, and our outings together, it would be hard for me to know how much money actually went to our weekend trip and how much went to his wrestling match. It's too broad a category for my life.

If you find yourself spending a lot of money on one particular item (shoes, for instance, or tickets to your favorite team's games), that's a sign you might want to create a budget category just for that item. Without those purchases hiding among other purchases, you can moderate your spending and see it more clearly.

If you have too many categories, you might not know how much to budget for it each paycheck. If you spend forty dollars this month on electronics but then don't spend in that category for another six months, it's not helpful to you to be budgeting for electronics every month. Try grouping it with a larger category.

This is a moment for you to make a judgment call and trust yourself.

Don't worry about budgeting a number for each of these categories yet. You will do that when we create your budget together later. For now, you just need to identify how you are spending your money. Just take a first stab at creating a set of categories.

Step 3: Get Curious about Your Spending

Now that you have a solid understanding of how much money you're spending and what kinds of things you're spending it on, it's time to ask the tough questions: In what situations do you spend often? What does your tracking reveal about each dimension of money for you? Are you balanced? Where do you spot an imbalance? Can you trace that imbalance back to life experiences or childhood money beliefs?

Take time to journal, reflect, and talk this through with someone who knows you well. How does what you've found make you feel?

It's not an easy task. During this process, negative feelings *will* surface. You might feel shame or guilt about your spending habits. You might feel fear about the future or what your spending says about you.

I've been there. It's uncomfortable. Shame and guilt can feel overwhelming. But if you can withstand it, the negative feelings will diminish and on the other side is a feeling of power and progress and confidence and conviction.

When I started studying these dimensions during my accreditation program, I immediately recognized myself: I was that compulsive spender who didn't value saving for the future. Fortunately, my relationship with money has changed over time; now, I'm balanced. I'm not a compulsive overspender, but I'm not a super-thrifty spender, either. I bring value into my life on a budget that I can afford.

For example, I used to buy all of my purses at Ross or T.J.Maxx because that's where I could find the best deal. But because I'm a mom who carries the entire kitchen sink in my bag, the low-quality fabrics would give out quickly. In a matter of a year, my purse would be in pretty poor condition. So, off I went, year after year, right back down to Ross to buy another one. It might seem budget friendly, but the frequency with which I needed to replace them meant it wasn't *really*.

Today, however, I take a different approach: I'll purchase one high-quality bag that I've saved up for and have it last me many years, rather than buy a bunch of inexpensive ones I'll have to replace soon.

This underlines an important facet of the Budget by Paycheck system: it's not about deprivation, but about thoughtful investment. I won't tell you that you can't buy a designer purse. If that's where you find *value*, you absolutely can; it may just be on a different timeline. Not everyone cares so much about how they carry around their things, but this is about figuring out what you *do* care about and then planning for ways to attain it.

That's balance.

Balance has transformed not just my purse collection, but my entire life. How did I get there? The very first step was in identifying the money messages I received as a child, identifying the significant life events that shaped my view of money, and being honest with myself about how I felt about money. Only then could I begin to see reality, and only then could I start planning for the reality I wanted—not the one I had found myself in.

My client Kate had a similar experience. She arrived at my office late one afternoon to show me her spending and create her budget. I had asked her to track her spending, as I normally do; it's the first step toward bringing awareness to your spending habits (and the slap-in-the-face moment that so many of us need).

As I was reviewing her purchases, an unusual pattern caught my eye. This darling woman had racked up thousands of dollars on credit cards buying the most unexpected accessory: nail polish.

I had to point out to her that it's unusual, to say the least, to spend that much money on nail polish. And when I asked her why she collected it, she couldn't answer me. "I don't know, I just have always had this thing for nail polish," she replied. "I've just always wanted my nails to look nice."

I suspected there was a buried reason, a hidden wound, behind these purchases, so I kept asking questions. She started talking and, sure enough, out of our conversation came this story of a young girl who, in middle school, was made to feel not good enough. "I was sitting at my desk," she shared, "and the girl in front of me looked down and said, 'God! You have really ugly nails!'" And the moment stuck with her subconscious.

What she internalized from that experience was that having perfect nails was the way to win others' approval. From that moment on, she always made sure to have these perfectly painted nails.

Maybe she had no idea how much she was actually spending on nail polish; nine dollars a pop doesn't *seem* like that much in isolated buying environments. But once we started tracking her spending, we saw just how much this addiction was costing her—to the tune of $400 a year.

Get curious about your spending and maintain a nonjudgmental mind-set. Ask yourself, "What does this spending say about me?"

Getting to the Heart of the Issue

So many of us try to address the symptom of "spending too much" without getting to the root of *why*. We search the internet for how to stop impulse buying. We read things like how to make a list when you go to the store. You might be familiar with the common tips: budget beforehand, avoid the mall, stop using your credit card. But for many, those "tips and tricks" ring hollow; it's all just "robot work." "Make a grocery list" won't help you in the long run if you can't see why you're spending money on things *off* your shopping list in the first place.

When you stay in the dark, it's all too easy to spend more than you make and dig yourself further into debt. And worse, it'll be impossible to foster a healthy relationship with money if you're oblivious to the one you have now. You'll stay stuck in the same relationship patterns, frustrated about why you're experiencing the same problems over and over. And that's because you can't change what you don't know. You *have* to be honest with yourself, not only about what you're spending money on but also why. Then, what started as a slap in the face turns out to be the key to moving toward what you really want in life.

What happens when you get real about where you're at? What happens when you take a hard look at the underlying, emotional causes of your spending? You have information. You get to know yourself. You're able to make better decisions about the things that matter to you, and how you should spend on them. And most importantly, you'll be able to trust yourself.

Thinking back to the time I spent trying to be Melanie Griffith, I know that coming face-to-face with my own spending habits helped me go from someone spending money to becoming someone else, to someone spending money to becoming a better version of *myself.* Learning to love myself, and everything that came with the real woman that I genuinely was, was perhaps one of the greatest fringe benefits of developing a healthy relationship with money. By recognizing and being truthful to myself about my spending issues—including why I spent money I didn't have—I was able to address the real problems in my life that were keeping me from happiness and self-acceptance.

One of the best things I did was picking up long-distance running to help with my spending triggers. When I was feeling bad about myself, instead of going to the mall or spending money, I would throw on a pair of running shoes and go for a jog. I started embracing natural beauty. It's why I don't wear makeup. It's why I don't make trips to the hair salon every three months, or feel the need to have the most popular clothes. It's why I do my own nails at home.

The knowledge that I would always be *the same me* no matter what I purchased gave me a power over my spending that I'd never experienced. It freed me from my spending cycles that were suddenly so clear.

I have learned to love myself for who I am and be genuinely comfortable in my own skin—and that inner confidence was born from the mental confidence I gained around money. (Turns out, money guilt can really seep into other areas of your life.)

Next up, it's time to build yours.

Make It Happen

Track Your Spending for a Month

Manually track your spending for an entire month. Download my expense tracker and print it out. Write down every time you spend money.

If you don't want to wait, pull statements from the last month—also pull credit card statements and report cash spending. Track all areas of money movement in your life.

Identify Spending Categories

Use my highlighter method to group like expenses together.

Tally each category for the month.

What surprised you about your spending habits?

Journal about the earliest messages you received about money: How did your parents handle money? Did you think about money as a kid? What did your parents teach you about money?

Journal about the life events that shape your view of money: What happened as you took control of your own finances? What happened in your personal life that affected your wallet?

For Those Following along with
the Budget by Paycheck Method

Go to Step #2: Track and categorize your spending in your *Budget by Paycheck® Workbook.*

Part Two

Make It Happen

CHAPTER SIX

Discover Your True Priorities (When Everything Feels Important)

The Budget Mom Family member Tammie came from an abusive household. She left home at age nineteen and juggled minimum-wage jobs and poor mental health for over a decade. Fighting just to cover her bills day by day, Tammie didn't have time to think about luxuries like "the future."

Unfortunately—as Tammie soon discovered—even if you aren't planning for the future, the future happens anyway. Before she knew it, she was married, then divorced, then $50,000 in debt . . . all while earning a minimal hourly wage.

Cue the decision to try to find her purpose in life. Having suffered for years in an unfulfilling job, Tammie decided to start her own business as an office organizer, and she taught herself QuickBooks. On top of that, she went after a college degree in 2002, funded totally by grants.

Then she had her son. She needed more room for her and her baby, so she moved to a bigger apartment, increasing her rent to $1,300—a steal in her city of Los Angeles. However, that was still over half of her monthly income, and soon her business wasn't bringing in enough money to cover the bills. Thirty-seven years old and left with no choice, she rejoined corporate America. She was laid off from corporate jobs three times during the 2008 to 2009 recession. After the last layoff, she moved in with family in Sacramento. Leaving her friends behind caused a deep depression.

Now a single mom with no real plan, she moved in with her father and relied on food stamps, unemployment, and child support to care for herself and her son. Eventually the child support stopped coming in and her depression got stronger. She slept most of the day, stressing about money. When she was awake, she worried about whether her car would start or whether her bank account was overdrawn.

But during this time, something good started to happen. Her father is a mindful spender and aggressive saver—and someone who knows his priorities. When saving for a vacation, he'll remind his family they must make trade-offs. "Do you want to go to Disney later, or to the movies and miniature golf now?" he'd ask. Soon, Tammie began to mimic his habits—as an adult, she could see their value—and began to make different priorities. The day she moved out of her father's house, she had paid off all of her debt, had a part-time job as a bookkeeper, and decided she was ready to rebuild her business.

Priorities not only give us direction, they give us confidence. As things looked up, she began to actually *believe* that she could create a better life for herself instead of operating in victim mode. For the first time ever, she asked herself what she wanted her life to look like in the future, instead of just suffering the consequences of what it was at the moment.

She envisioned that she and her son would one day have a comfortable home, a stocked fridge, a savings account, and the ability to help her friends as they'd helped her.

The first breakthrough was realizing that she had to prioritize stabilizing her income. Because Tammie was a part-time worker with multiple jobs, her income was variable. This had always held her back from proper planning.

Once her job was secure, however, she set up automatic payments for her bills so she didn't have to stress when they were due. By the time she found *The Budget Mom*, she was already using the cash envelope method, cashless method, and sinking funds. But becoming a part of the Budget Mom Family forced her to take a step back and look at all of the progress she'd made. After seventeen years of struggle, she had paid off $50,000 worth of debt.

While there are habits that might hold us back from spending money wisely, there is also no one "right way" to spend. Because everyone's lives are different, everyone is going to have different priorities when it comes to spending. What's important is that you spend on what *you* value— and to finally be able to afford what *you* need.

But, where do you start?

Because money touches every part of your life, you'll quickly find that the options for what you *could* do with your money is endless: invest, save for small purchases, put money toward retirement, prepare for your child's future, save for emergencies. The list goes on.

Worse, it ALL feels important. You want to save for a car, but you also want to pay off debt. You want to be able to retire by sixty, but you also want to go on a vacation this year. You want to be able to afford the surprise dentist bill, but you also want to save for your child's college education.

When you feel overwhelmed by the options, you can easily spread yourself too thin: you save for a bunch of different little things, and then hardly see progress. Or maybe you save in only one area, making it all but impossible not to fall back on your credit card when emergencies strike. It's defeating to try to make progress but keep falling into the same patterns. You might end up thinking to yourself, "Is it even worth trying?"

The first step out of the confusion and overwhelm (and not relying forever on your credit card for emergencies) is to get clear on your *personal financial priorities*. As soon as Tammie figured out what hers were—stabilizing her income—everything started to fall into place. Over the next few years, she used the methods that worked for her to build a life she loves on a budget she can afford. (That part is key.) Today, at fifty-two years old, she owns an established bookkeeping business, which she bought in cash. She's using her tried-and-true system to save for a store and other operating expenses, and homeownership is on the horizon as her son plans to go to college in the next few years.

You, too, can build a life you love—but first you've got to figure out what you need.

Where to Start: Your Emergency Fund

I can't tell you what your priorities are, but I can guarantee that life will hit you with unexpected expenses—and those surprises will come sooner than you'd like. Before I walk you through your prioritization process, I want to make sure you have your bases covered so that life doesn't derail you on the path to reaching your goals.

You've heard financial experts since the beginning of time tell you that you need an emergency fund—and I agree. Unlike sinking funds, which are for planned expenses and savings goals, **an emergency fund is for an unexpected, unplanned event in your life**. It's for when someone breaks their arm or for when the car battery dies. This money is not budgeted for anything else; it just sits in your bank account until you need it.

An emergency fund is always a short-term goal. (Don't wait three years to make it; life's emergencies won't wait!) But saving for an emergency fund doesn't simply mean saving an arbitrary $1,000 and moving on; you need to have enough to truly cover you, you know, *in the event of an emergency*. Therefore, as a starting point, I recommend taking your necessary expenses and multiplying them by three. That's your goal. Write down the number.

You may, however, want to save even more than that. For me, when I first started on this journey, I needed much more than $1,000 in the bank to feel comfortable—especially in case anything were to happen to my son. So I set a short-term goal of $3,000 as my emergency fund. Three thousand dollars may sound like a lot. It certainly was for me at the time. I couldn't do it in one paycheck. That's why I had to begin with what I call a **"kickoff" emergency fund**.

A kickoff emergency fund is an amount that is achievable for you in just one to two months. If that amount is $200, that's fine. You'll add to it later, but for now just "kick off" with what you can afford with the dollars that you have. This is part one of your emergency fund savings.

The reason I believe in a kickoff emergency fund is that when you have never saved before, saving the smallest amount can seem impossible, until it's not. Start by proving to yourself that you can save, even if it's not the entire emergency fund that you will need.

Part two is the rest of what you need to feel safe and cover necessary living expenses. After you've hit your achievable kickoff emergency fund, then you can put money aside every paycheck toward your emergency fund as part of one of your first short-term goals.

When do you use your emergency fund? It's important to remember that an emergency fund is only for emergencies. It's *not* for eating out or for a weekend trip with the girls. It's for those unexpected times life hits you over the head.

I recently dipped into my emergency fund because my AC unit broke in my brand-new house. Just because something is "new" doesn't mean it won't break. Your emergency fund is a line item you never get rid of. And then, when you use it, you can slowly put money toward it to build it back up again over time.

You might be wondering where you put your emergency fund: a checking account? A savings account? Should you invest it? People wonder, "Couldn't I be earning a better return on it if I invested it?"

An emergency fund should be something that you have immediate access to, and therefore I never recommend investing that safety net. No CDs at the bank, not even a higher yield online savings account. Often, with online savings accounts, you have to wait one to two days to withdraw your money if you don't have a checking account established at the same institution—and it's far more with invested money. What if something happens and you need that money before two days to two weeks? If it's truly an emergency, chances are you'll need the money right away. That money should be there for you when you really need it, so my advice is to hold it in a traditional savings account at your regular bank, something that you have immediate access to. If you have a larger emergency fund, I think it's fine to put some of it in a high-yield savings account. But make sure you keep some as immediately accessible cash, like in that regular savings account at your banking institution.

An emergency fund is an important short-term goal, but it's not all you need to be saving for.

What Makes a Priority a Priority? Wants versus Needs

Once your emergency savings is fully funded, you can start to tackle the financial priorities that feel completely personal to you. **Your financial priorities are your big-picture budgeting items, the goals you want to accomplish over time.** They might even seem out of reach right now, but that's okay: we're going to get you there!

When you're imagining your big-picture priorities, try to steer away from smaller savings items like new jeans or dinner out. Your financial priorities are your debt payments and your savings goals, everything that you can't simply use the money coming in from this month's paycheck to cover. Without becoming crystal clear on these priorities, you will end up spending money on activities that aren't actually close to your heart. Then, you won't have money for what really matters, and you'll end up relying on debt—again—because you were not prepared.

When you are struggling to cover your bills, everything feels important and it's difficult to prioritize. But the good news is this: it's never too early to decide what you want in life. And the very first step is figuring out the difference between your "wants" and your "needs."

Without confusing the two.

It's difficult to define a need, but it's easy to identify when our needs aren't getting met. If you neglect a need, your life likely falls into chaos until you meet that need. Even small needs can really dictate how your day goes: a way to get to work, a sitter for your children, getting dinner on the table, taking your prescription, etc.

Wants are different. You will always have more of them than you can afford. Your "wants" could be small things, like another swimsuit, or it could be something big, like a certain kind of house or car. If you want to be content and secure financially, you have to identify the wants that are the most important to you and the ones you can live without.

No one else can decide what a want or a need is for you. Your needs—for your physical body, for your emotional health, for your family and living situation—are unique to you. But here are a few of the questions I ask myself to distinguish my own wants from my own needs:

How does this expense benefit my life?

Is this something that can wait?

Is there a less expensive version of this?

What would be the sacrifice of spending money on an alternative?

Will there be consequences if I don't spend money on this?

If there are big consequences for *not* having the money for something, then likely it falls into the category of a need. Needs must come first. Categories like housing, transportation, insurance, and retirement are mission critical. If we have our wants fulfilled, but not our needs, life goes into chaos. Think of the consequences of NOT meeting a need and prioritize accordingly to severity of consequence.

How to Prioritize: Short-, Medium-, and Long-term Goals

The key to prioritizing is to assign a timeline to your goals: short, medium, and long term. These are the stepping-stones on your financial journey. Paying off debt can be a short-, medium-, or long-term goal that you work on while accomplishing other goals.

Short-term goals are your most urgent financial goals, what you want to achieve within one to three years. Maybe you have a health procedure you've been putting off, like a dentist visit. Maybe your child has tuition due each semester. Maybe you need a reliable vehicle to get to work. Maybe it's your student or credit card debt (if one to three years seems like a manageable payoff time). When you hit the end of three years—or reach your short-term goals—you pass a significant mile marker and move on to medium-term goals.

Medium-term goals are not as urgent as short-term goals, though they're still important. These goals support your bigger, long-term goals, and usually take between three and seven years to accomplish. These goals look a little bit into the future: Perhaps you want to save for a house. Maybe you want to pay off debt, or save for college. Only you can know what will take you three to seven years to accomplish, given your current income.

Long-term goals, on the other hand, are your biggest, most ambitious goals. They are what you want to achieve in seven to ten or more years. For long-term goals, try to aim as high as you can possibly imagine. The temptation here is to hold ourselves back: Too often, we discount ourselves and say, "I'll never get that." Maybe "that" is a house or a certain salary. Maybe it's an early retirement. Maybe it's just becoming debt-free.

Hear me when I say it's possible for you. The amount of money you make right now isn't a limitation to how much you *can* earn—or how big you can dream. It is far better to aim too high than to never aim anywhere at all. Never, ever discount yourself. Dream big and go for it! The financial foundations you learn in this book will keep you steady throughout your journey.

You'll find that even quickly separating your priorities this way will help ease your mind. You've got focus! Your short-term (one-to-three-year) goals are your first priorities. Those need to be met before you hit your medium-term goals. And those medium-term goals (three to seven years) need to be met before you hit the long-term goals (seven to ten-plus years). And voilà, the sorting has done itself.

Little Progress over a Long Time: Sinking Funds

It's intimidating to look at all of the goals at the same time and think, "I need $20,000? That's so much money, I'm never going to get there!" That's why it's helpful to break down our big goals into manageable chunks. We'll talk more about making your goals achievable when we set a realistic budget (a later foundation). But right now, I want you to start practicing goal setting immediately. Enter sinking funds.

A sinking fund is for a planned, expected event in your life. A sinking fund is a strategic way to save a little bit of every paycheck to pay for planned large expenses. Sinking funds are useful for those important, expected expenses for which you are saving in the short term (one to three years). Again, maybe it's tuition or a recreational expense like a sports league. Maybe it's something fun like a vacation. The idea of a sinking fund is something that you put small increments toward

over time. Instead of paying it all at once, you will have saved for an event you know is coming.

Think about the past three years. Was there one annually recurring event when you felt pressured to use your credit card? Was there a time in those years when you had to pull out your credit card over and over again?

For many people I talk to, that event is Christmas. We'll get into why we fall into the same patterns of spending, over and over again, later in the book (hint: it has way more to do with our emotions than it has to do with our reasoning), but right now let's agree that the holiday season is a biggie that pulls at our heartstrings. On top of the emotion of the season, there are a bunch of sales to tempt you, making it (dangerously) easy to put thousands of dollars on your credit card.

For years, I did the same thing. December was the time of year I felt the most dread: I felt hopeless and defeated with my finances. But the reality is I knew Christmas was coming. It comes every year.

So I started a sinking fund for Christmas. In the beginning, I kept the total goal low: about $200. Over the year, I saved for that $200 in small increments so it didn't feel like a huge hit to my budget. It wasn't taking away too much from my other savings goals, but it was just enough to set aside something where I could be prepared with cash.

Christmas is a great example, but it's not just the small goals that you can do this with; you can also use this same method for longer-term savings goals.

1. List the goal you want to save for.

2. Determine a specific amount to save.

3. Give the goal a deadline (a goal date).

4. Write down any money you have already saved for that specific goal.

5. Take your goal amount and subtract it from the money you have already saved (if you have saved anything for that goal). This will give you the amount you still need to save.

6. Take the amount you need to save and divide it by the number of months you have to save. This gives you the amount you need to save every month to reach your savings goal by your goal deadline (goal date).

If you want to save $5,000, ask yourself how you will mark your progress. Maybe it's a tracker sheet or even a sticky note on a bulletin board. Are you setting up small tasks to support that goal? Maybe that means transferring $100 to your savings each week, or maybe that means setting a reminder to do it manually. Any small action that can be checked off is going to help you with this process.

Reaching even big money goals is possible, and sinking funds are a great tool to help you get there. Think of each savings goal as a springboard: Each time you reach a goal, you build up financial confidence. Each time you reach that goal, you feel more motivated.

Managing Multiple Goals: The Myth of "All or Nothing"

It's true that the fastest way to make progress on a particular goal is to put all of your excess money toward that goal. That's why so many financial experts stress choosing one goal and sticking to it. For example, getting rid of debt first before saving for any other goals (even retirement) is common advice.

However, I disagree that you should save for only one goal, sacrificing all others until that one is finished.

Take, for example, someone who wants to pay off debt. For the last year, she's made debt the priority. She's put a lot of money toward it but still has a long way to go. The problem is, she just recently found out she is pregnant, and realizes she'll need to take some unpaid time off for maternity leave. Naturally, she needs to have enough money to cover expenses during that time.

This is a great example of why it's important to save for more than one goal at a time. Yes, this might mean paying off the debt a little slower, but it also means not going into new debt because you're now financially prepared for maternity leave. Paying off debt is a medium-term goal, whereas saving for maternity leave is an immediate short-term goal. It's the short-term goal that has priority, and your spending should reflect that.

After she's saved enough for the maternity leave, then she can return to paying off debt. Done this way, her priorities take turns and, over the course of the year, she makes significant progress on both goals.

Just because you value a long-term goal doesn't mean you have to put money toward it every single month. You *can* hit pause. This doesn't make you a bad or irresponsible person. The opposite is true: it makes you flexible and strategic. To save for only one big goal (for instance, debt) might force you to put off other goals that will bring significant value to your life.

More than just being manageable, saving for multiple goals is often necessary. Life comes in and throws you curveballs, like flooded basements or a family wedding. The truth is, it's rare NOT to save for multiple goals at once. And it's *also* rare to have enough money to save for all of our wants and needs—which means priorities are more important than ever.

Having a strong foundation isn't just about learning how to save for one thing but knowing how to tackle more than one financial goal at a time. Knowing how to prioritize where you put your money is one of the most important financial planning decisions you will have to make.

Without naming it, I've just introduced a concept that has helped me, time and time again, make tough decisions—and one I use almost every day in financial counseling: trade-offs. Just like Tammie's dad used.

A trade-off is when you make a specific sacrifice for the sake of being able to afford something else. When we're calculating what we can afford, we make trade-offs all the time. I don't know how many times I've gone to the store and thought, "I'd like to get both of these items, but I can only afford one. Which should I choose?" We sacrifice the chili cheese fries for the ice cream cone. We sacrifice the pink sweater for the red one.

But it's more than these small sacrifices. I want you to think in terms of your actual goals. Because money spent in one area means that you cannot use that same money toward your other priorities. In the example above, the woman preparing for maternity leave makes a trade-off: she puts money there that she would have normally put toward debt. When you or I spend money on something like dinner out, we cannot use that twenty dollars on something like a down payment.

It doesn't make it wrong to go out to eat, but it always requires a trade-off.

We trick ourselves into thinking that, when we spend money, we're not giving up anything, that we can afford the credit card purchase and still have money for going out to dinner. But the truth is that we're *always* making sacrifices, even when we don't realize it. Most often, when we're closing our eyes to consequences, it's because we're creating more debt for ourselves and sacrificing our future. We end up having to put off things like home ownership or retirement or even that vacation we wanted. But that's not what we thought about when we used our credit cards. **However, every dollar spent is a sacrifice on some other budget line.**

But trade-offs are actually part of our power; we get to choose which sacrifices we want to make. Is your son having a memorable Christmas with lots of presents this year more important than saving for his college? You have to look at it that way. And there's not a right answer! Perhaps, like in my situation, your family just went through a really bad divorce. Your son had a rough year. Maybe it's worth it to you to put off some tuition to have an extra-special Christmas this season. What's most important is that you make the decision with *eyes wide open.*

When you look at everything you want to do, you might feel like it's all equally important. But in reality, it's not. You know in your heart what's more important to you. If someone came to you and said, "You have five seconds to choose between this goal and that goal, or I'm taking away all your money," I guarantee you would choose one thing or another. Even if the two goals felt similarly important, one thing would jump out; that's what's more important to you.

Or, if you don't want to go with your gut, try using chronology, prioritizing short-term goals first. You can also trade off percentages. Say you want to start paying off debt while also saving for your emergency fund. You can choose that! Perhaps 70 percent of your extra income goes toward debt and the rest goes to your emergency fund. You won't make progress as fast on either one (and I do suggest having one be a "higher" priority), but it works. You still do have to make a trade-off, but that doesn't mean it always has to be an either-or. It can be an "and."

And remember, the goals you choose to work toward are *FINE.*

There's no such thing as "a goal you're not supposed to be working toward right now." There is no predetermined list of what's okay and not okay to prioritize. You're in control; you get to decide what trade-offs you want to make. And everything you do from here on out is better than nothing.

Prioritization: A Case Study

Let's say that Wanda has identified three financial goals she wants to tackle, and she's labeled them according to when she needs the money.

Short-term goal: Christmas—$300 in four months

Medium-term goal: New car down payment—$4,000 in nine months

Long-term goal: New house down payment—$25,000 in four years

To break down how much she needs to save for each goal each month, we divide the total by the number of months she has to save.

For Christmas, she would need to save $75 per month ($300 ÷ 4)

For the car, she would need to save $445 per month ($4,000 ÷ 9)

For the house down payment, she would need to save $521 per month ($25,000 ÷ 4 ÷ 12)

Now that's a lot of money every month—about $1,041 per month to save. But the problem is, Wanda only has $500 per month to throw at her financial goals. So Wanda has to use trade-offs to determine when she's saving for which goal.

When you're saving for multiple things at once, rely on chronology. Usually, short-term goals are smaller value than long- or even medium-term goals. So if you tackle them in chronological order, short term to long term, you can fulfill the short-term goal first and then give the long-term goal a turn as priority number one.

For Wanda, this means the following:

Month 1: $300 to Christmas, $200 to her car

Months 2 to 8: $500 to her car

Month 9: $300 to car, $200 to her down payment

Month 10 and beyond: $500 toward her down payment

Therefore, if she only has $500 every month to put toward her financial goals, and she tackles them based on her priorities and in chronological order, then the first month she would fund her Christmas goal in its entirety—$300—and would then put the other $200 toward the new car. Woo, one goal fulfilled! Then, over the next seven months, she would put the entire $500 toward the car, since that's her medium-term goal. By month nine, she would have funded her car goal with $300, and then she would put the other $200 toward her house down payment. Wanda can then focus and spend the entire $500 on her house down payment goal, getting her pretty close to fulfilling all three goals (and making a smart, organized plan to do so!).

In the end, she won't quite have saved up enough for the $25,000 down payment in four years, but she'll be close to $20,000. She will then have to stay in her current accommodations for four more years, but that might be a trade-off she wants to make. She might decide it's worth it to have a nice Christmas and push back the new house down payment.

In my Budget Mom Family, we often talk through trade-offs and sinking funds. In scrolling through the comments and the discussion, what you will find is that priorities are unique to each person. Some are saving for annual vacations or birthdays. Some keep sinking funds for kids, clothing, or eye care. Grace shares about how she and her partner used to just "hope" that they had enough money when expenses came around. "For the first time, I feel prepared," she said.

Sometimes, however, you will spend money outside of your priorities. Sometimes, you'll find yourself in a pinch and spend money eating out. Or maybe two emergencies hit at once. Maybe you find yourself splurging at the mall. Whatever you do, don't get down on yourself when life happens. The financial foundations I'm offering in this book will help you create a life that is stable enough to handle occasional spending outside of your priorities. When you're tempted to feel guilty, try to reframe it. Did you spend cash instead of relying on credit? Then count that as a win.

Make It Happen

Make a list of all your possible priorities.

Ask yourself, "What are my most important financial goals?"

Ask yourself, "What am I willing to give up to reach these goals?"

Divide these priorities into time segments.

What can you accomplish (or what do you need to accomplish) in one to three years? If you don't have an emergency fund, make it a goal, here.

What can you accomplish (or what do you need to accomplish) in three to seven years?

What can you accomplish (or what do you need to accomplish) in seven to ten-plus years?

For Those Following along with the Budget by Paycheck Method

Go to Step #6: Prioritize your savings goals.

CHAPTER SEVEN

A Budget for Your Real Life, Not the "Perfect" Version

W hen my client Casey first came into my office, she was nearly in tears. She had recently divorced her husband and was restructuring her entire life, including her finances. She had tried *so hard* to budget the traditional way, making a list of all her bills, racking her brain for every single envelope she got in the mail, noting down every payment: her car, her community college tuition, her electricity bills. She did the math in her head: "It should work," she thought. "I have just enough."

And it was critical that she had enough. Casey had two daughters to take care of, all on her own.

But three months later, by the time she came into my office, Casey was defeated. Despite working full time as a receptionist and taking on part-time weekend work, she was still relying on her credit card to get by every month. She looked at me in desperation, and said, "I just don't know what to do! I keep writing it all out, and it all works on paper, but then it never seems to actually *work.*"

As Casey and I talked further, however, I spotted the problem right away. It's a classic mistake, one I see people make over and over again.

The one gigantic factor that she and so many others fail to consider: real life.

When I say the word "budget," what comes to mind? Perhaps it's a spreadsheet with line items and numbers. Maybe it's a pile of bills. Maybe it paints a picture of a tightfisted penny-pincher, splitting hairs over who owes what on the check at Applebee's.

Most people have a very stereotypical idea of what a budget is, categories of spending and set "rules" on how much you can spend, and on what. The goal is to spend less than you make by planning beforehand how much money goes where. And that sounds reasonable! Sure. Even noble.

But it's not realistic.

Casey's challenges with her budget happened because she was equating her budget with bill paying. Many people assume that if they list every bill, they'll have accounted for everything. The rest of the money becomes "spending" money—money that isn't tracked and, often, disappears quickly.

So what happens when Casey wants to go out with one of her work friends for lunch? What happens when one of her daughters comes home from school with a soccer tournament on the calendar? What happens when the other daughter wants to go to a birthday party, or another mom in the class asks for someone to bring snacks for a school event?

A Budget for Your Real Life, Not the "Perfect" Version

That's Casey's real life, one with activities and events and daily unplanned occurrences. And all of these things cost money. So when Casey keeps her budget confined to her bills, she's actually only budgeted for *some* of the things she needs to. Then the other expenses pop up and whisper, "Boo," sending her best-laid plans into a spiral.

Paying your bills on time is only 50 percent of the strategy. But your bills are not the reason for your budget; your budget is there to help you manage your life. Gracefully and thoughtfully, with ease, joy, and calm. Otherwise, it's a useless exercise in vanity. Paying your bills on time *is* important, of course, but a great budget also incorporates the fun—and realistic—parts of your life: birthdays, holidays, meals out, a new pair of pants from Zara. Your real life is more than just your bills, and your budget has to account for it all.

That said, I want to take the next three chapters to talk about creating and sticking to a budget that works for your *real* life, one that considers both where you are (financial awareness) and where you want to go (your financial goals). I want to empower you to create something sustainable and powerful and forward-thinking so you can live a life you love without feeling like you've got to punish yourself for the one you have.

And as you might have guessed, we aren't just going to account for your monthly bills but will also incorporate every part of your financial life: the good, the bad, the ugly, *and* the beautiful.

This foundation is one I'm particularly passionate about. It revolutionized budgeting for me, helping it all *finally* make sense.

It's called the Budget Calendar.

How to Create a Budget Calendar

Your budget calendar is your financial road map that helps you navigate your real life and sets you up for budgeting success.

A budget calendar is just like your regular calendar, but with the single purpose of keeping track of your finances. While we'll surely also be tracking the standard items such as your bill due dates, mortgage or rent payments, income, and savings amounts to help you see what's coming in and going out, we will also be using this calendar to help you plan for life events we sometimes forget about until it's too late—aka, the real life between the bills.

Step 1: Record Money Coming In

First, start with a fresh calendar and your income. On this fresh calendar, I want you to write down the amount you will be paid on the day you will get the money in your bank account. I like to mark it in big letters: PAYDAY.

Many of you have variable income: it fluctuates, depending on how many hours you work and how much your customers tip. In that case, I recommend budgeting according to the worst-case scenario, meaning the *least* possible amount of money in and the *most* possible money out. To be prepared for the worst, you have to plan for the worst, right? So, in this step, that means writing down the minimum amount of money you might receive. If you are guaranteed thirty hours a week, but might pick up more shifts, write down your thirty-hour-a-week paycheck amount, even if you hope to earn more. That way, if it happens that you log thirty hours, you won't have to rely on debt to make it through the month.

If you are paid daily (in cash tips, for example), you'll need to save up your daily income and use it only on your designated budget days. I know a lot of people in the service industry who rely on their tips to survive financially, and therefore their base paycheck just isn't enough. In this situation, use your base pay as the worst-case scenario. Write that on your calendar (on its appropriate pay date), and then use your calendar to log any daily income. Track your daily tip amount and then pick two designated budgeting days on your calendar. Save your tips daily until your budgeting day. This way, you know exactly how much income you are working with. On your designated budget days, bring all of your cash tips to the bank and deposit that cash into your checking account or the account that you use to pay your expenses.

At the end of this step, you'll know how much money you can count on (and when).

Step 2: Record Money Going Out

This is where your previous foundation of financial awareness becomes especially valuable. Look at the spending categories you've identified. In order to prepare for real life, *all* of these kinds of expenses belong on your calendar. Both looking at your spending and looking at the events on your calendar are exercises in awareness: in order to be prepared for your real-life expenses, you have to know your current real-life habits.

Refer to your expense worksheet and then put these expenses on your calendar according to each due date.

Fixed Expenses

- Same date, same amount payments like your housing, health insurance, phone bill, minimum debt payments, and automatic savings or investment contributions

- Semiannual, infrequent payments like homeowner's insurance, vehicle registration, website subscriptions, quarterly insurance, and gym memberships

Fixed expenses are consistent bills and payments; it's the rent, the car payment, the internet bill. The stuff you (most likely) were already trying to budget for your first time around. They're any bill that charges around the same amount on a regular basis. On the day it is due, write down the amount you owe on your calendar.

Include also minimum debt payments and any automatic savings or investment contributions and when you plan to pay those. You may end up being able to make bigger payments (hopefully you can!) but first, you have to know the minimum amount.

Variable Expenses

• Same date, varying amount payments like utilities and credit cards

• Varying date, varying amount payments like groceries and gasoline

Variable expenses are the most unpredictable expenses and, because of that, are the hardest to budget for. Variable costs are expenses not set in stone. The dollar amount they cost us—each week or month—depends on the week or month. You have more control over how much you spend in these categories, whether that's how much you drive your car or how long you run the AC, or if you decide to eat expensive steak or just survive on ramen noodles.

Tip: I always recommend that you also use the worst-case scenario when it comes to estimating your variable expenses. This means, for the varying payments, always *over*estimate. For example, if your utility bill runs around $133, write down and budget for $140.

The point is not to guess how little you could spend (a common error); it's to estimate how much you will actually spend and prepare for that number. Use your knowledge of your spending trends (your financial awareness) to help you make an educated guess. Then, if you do end up spending less, you'll have more money for other financial goals. (Yay!)

For variable expenses that do not have a set due date (e.g., you're not sure yet which day you will go grocery shopping for the week)—simply pick one. I suggest the beginning of the month or the week, depending on how often you use this category.

Events on the Calendar

- Birthdays, holidays, coffee, savings, etc.

My schedule helps me determine which holidays or special events I need to prepare for and gives me an estimate of how much I need to save. This is when having a calendar in front of you is really helpful. I suggest looking at the entire year (no matter where you are in the year, start preparing for one year out). The first thing I do is go month by month and write down every major holiday. I then write down recurring birthdays that I spend money on year after year. Next, I write down any known occasions that will be happening. I explained sinking funds in the last chapter: make sure these are on your calendar. For example, if I know a friend is getting married in June, I will write down their wedding date on my calendar. Do you have a family member that is graduating in the New Year? Any event or holiday that you spend money on throughout the year should be written down on your calendar. Plain and simple.

Alongside my calendar, I also use a yearly savings goal and event worksheet and tracker. But, again, even if you don't use my worksheets, the principle is the same: For sinking funds, break down the end goal into monthly payments. To get to $200 by Christmas, how much do you need to save per month? To get to $300 by the wedding in July, how

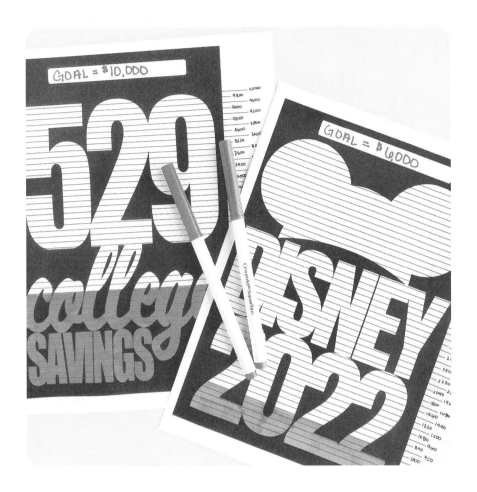

much are you going to save each month? Take your goal amount and divide that number by the number of months you have to save.

Get especially detailed about the few months ahead of you. Write down every event you can think of: your doctor appointments, haircuts, school field trips, lunches, friend dates, workshops, and tournaments. Make sure that everything you are spending money on is written down on your calendar. You'll be surprised just how much everyday activities cost! I like to use different colored markers for events and appointments, grouped by kind. Let your organizational self go wild. Add stickers or goal reminders, or little doodles designating different categories.

Other Savings Goals

- Savings goals like your emergency fund, medical deductibles, car savings, and extra debt payments.

You might not consider "savings" an expense, but that's just what it is! You are making a conscious decision to save money now so you can spend it later. This goes on your calendar! Whether you're saving for that emergency fund or have other sinking funds, such as your next phone, put that on your calendar, too. It feels like a lot, but I promise that it will actually relieve stress in the end.

At this point, it's normal to not know exactly how much you'll be able to put toward each savings goal (and that amount might vary from month to month). For now, put it on the calendar, but leave the amount blank.

Now, compare: Double-check your list by reviewing your spending log and the budget categories you made from your spending (foundation #2). Is anything missing? Review to be sure you're covering all your real-life expenses. Remember to factor in the little things like your biweekly latte, your monthly pickup at the dry cleaners, or your Friday work lunches. These are regular expenses that add up quickly and make more of an impact than you realize. Remember, awareness is power.

Step 3: Budget by Paycheck

This step is where my entire budgeting method gets its name. It's a step I'm super excited to show you. For me, this was my big aha moment. Budgeting—in all its complex glory—finally made sense.

A Budget for Your Real Life, Not the "Perfect" Version

You see, typical advice tells you to budget month to month. In fact, most of us just assume that's how it works: monthly. It asks you to list your monthly bills (remember what I said about bills!) and plan your expenses according to what you will spend that month. However, as we saw with Casey—and as I once experienced firsthand myself—this method almost guarantees that you'll end up relying on your credit cards to cover unanticipated expenses, and makes it difficult to actually accommodate the real world (and all of your changing needs).

Enter the Budget by Paycheck Method that I developed for myself out of necessity. Someone had to do *something*, because planning over the course of a month was too overwhelming, too prone to cracks and crevices I couldn't account for. There were too many variables in between—in other words, the real-world stuff—and so one day, as I was doing my budgeting, I had an aha moment:

If you get paid twice a month, why not budget twice a month?

So I tried it. Instead of trying to match my expenses with each month—an arbitrary measure of time—I decided to try matching my expenses with each paycheck. I began assigning specific expenses to specific paychecks, meaning I paid only *some* of my expenses with any given paycheck, leaving the others hanging—at least temporarily—until I got the second one. And then I'd re-budget my money every time I got paid, which was the fifth and the twentieth. Using this new system, I created and adjusted my budget twice a month, making it easier to keep a pulse on my real-time finances (instead of just flying blind for thirty days at a time). By making that one small adjustment, everything changed for me.

Today, many years later, I still budget by paycheck and use the Budget Calendar to help me plan out which expenses I want to pay with which paycheck. And let me tell you, it is so much easier. And so much more effective! I'm more in control of my money and can make decisions on the fly if I need to readjust in a category here or borrow from another category over there. (You know, for that girls' night out you shouldn't feel guilty for!)

This brings me to the final step of the Budget Calendar: matching expenses with your paycheck. Remember I mentioned color-coding your calendar, à la the highlighter method? This is where that really comes in handy. (It's a trillion times easier to see.) So here's what I want you to do:

All of the expenses that you pay with your paycheck on the fifth, highlight in pink on your calendar. All of the expenses that you pay with your paycheck on the twentieth, highlight in green (or whichever two colors you want). By using colors, you'll be able to quickly see which expenses still need to be paid, and with which paycheck.

Even if the category listed (clothing, beauty, eating out) doesn't have a dollar amount attached to it yet (just wait, that's the next foundation!), I still want you to match it with a paycheck. What the calendar helps us do is see how much money we have to spend on those variable expenses.

Make it a habit to revisit your calendar often, adding events as they come up and assigning them to a paycheck.

What to Do When You Come Up Short

As you start to compare your spending habits (aka your expense tracker categories) with your real life (your activities, bills, and actual paychecks), it's likely you'll find what I found: you're spending more than you make. You might get out the highlighters and do some quick math and find it's not adding up. Your income isn't covering what you're currently spending.

Ding, ding, ding! This is exactly where you *should* be at this point, grappling with the reality of just how much is coming in versus how much your lifestyle actually costs. But that's okay; no need to worry. The next foundation will help you use all this information—even the stuff you're loath to see—to create a budget that actually works.

Everything you've gathered so far—bills, variable expenses, due dates, sinking funds—will all come together on a single page: the Paycheck Budget Tracker. Or, if you don't prefer to use my worksheet, I encourage you to make one of your own. What's most important is that you match your actual expenses (from your actual life, not just your "in a perfect world, I'd only spend ten dollars on groceries" life) with your actual income.

Advantages of a Budget Calendar: Visual + Organized

The Budget Calendar sets you up for success, and I have actually come to enjoy making it. It's very similar to taking inventory of your food and making meal plans when you're trying to eat healthy. If you don't know what you have in the freezer and what to thaw out next, you're more likely to gravitate toward convenience and eat out.

Budget calendars keep you organized in the same way. Not only are they visually satisfying, but they help you manage your money, eliminate ugly surprises, and organize all of your finances in one place. They keep you focused on what's coming up, remind you when each bill needs to be paid, and save you from late fees. (Hallelujah.)

I suggest putting your calendar in a visible spot, preferably close to where you sit down to budget. Seeing it in front of you (something like a vision board!) is motivating.

The calendar will also help you find ways to streamline the process. Too many bills coming out at the first of the month? Ask for some of your due dates to change. (Yes! You can do that!) Utility companies and credit card lenders are usually very accommodating when it comes to adjusting payment dates. Too many bills of the same kind? Consider consolidating your credit card debt to a single card with a lower interest rate.

The Budget Calendar can help you see small debts that can be paid off and eliminated, and others that can be set up on an automatic draft from your bank so you never have to worry about them being overlooked.

Finally, the calendar helps you make a habit of saving. Like eating healthy, when you start to see the results, it motivates you to make adjustments and keep going. Likewise, when the bills are getting paid on time, money's going into savings, and your debt is decreasing, it's encouraging!

Nothing makes me happier than to see the hundreds of TBM Family members posting photos of their colorful budget calendars. People report on everything as small as withdrawing cash for coffee to saving for an expensive "dream" espresso maker.

Cherie wrote in and said, "I had no idea how often I was reaching for my credit card. Seeing it all laid out like this is so helpful!"

Sasha posted a picture of her calendar and proudly reported that she knew exactly what bills and what expenses came from each paycheck.

Sarah shared a point of celebration, sharing that she no longer had to rely on her parents for monthly expenses.

It's a great feeling to know exactly how you'll cover each expense.

The Case for Manual Budgeting

People ask me if it's worth printing out a calendar and writing everything out. They ask if it's okay if they use their Google Calendar, or their Apple Calendar app, or whatever one's right on their phone.

My answer is yes, but not at first.

Sure, you *could* use an electronic calendar. You can also use digital spreadsheets for your budget; there are plenty of templates out there on the internet for you to choose from, and there are plenty of online tools and apps you can pay for to help you organize your finances. They work for some people.

Even so, I always advocate for manual budgeting in the beginning, and that's because nothing can replace the financial clarity that comes from having to organize the money yourself. There it is. Tangible. In front of your face. Money you can organize with your hands. And it makes such a difference.

Do you have to be a manual budgeter forever? No. But I recommend it for people who are just starting my program—especially if you think you're "bad" at numbers. True financial awareness comes from doing this work: deciding on the categories that fit with your life, recording what you spend your money on, and matching a paycheck with each expense. If you don't record it manually, it's easy to become detached:

the money doesn't feel *real*. We separate ourselves from our money and neglect to see just how connected our lifestyles, emotions, and long hours at work are with the numbers we see on our bank statements.

For me, creating a budget calendar by hand and attaching each expense to a paycheck changed my life. I saw how my budget was working (or, at first, how it wasn't working!). I had put the same information, thousands of times, into digital programs. Why was this so different?

Well, studies show that actually putting pen to paper changes the way the human brain processes information; it helps us register it on a deeper level. Experts call it the generation effect. Go ahead, try to write something down and then think about something else while you're doing it. Can you? I bet it's difficult. When you physically write something, you have to focus on what you're writing, 100 percent. Writing is not an activity your body can do on autopilot; you can't mentally check out. Your mind has to be present and focused.

Therefore, writing down your budget manually will also help you process and store the information in a deeper, more meaningful way. It gets flagged as something important—and trust me, this information deserves to be front and center. To put it there, I suggest actually writing it down. (I promise I'm not just trying to torture you for fun.)

"Things Kept Popping Up"

I often hear from people that "things kept popping up." *Oh, life, how you love to derail our plans.*

However, I'm willing to bet that your life is more predictable than you might think. While it's true that sometimes expenses come out of nowhere, the thing about your life is that it's yours, and you're intimately acquainted. You know what you have coming up; look at that beautiful budget calendar we made you! You know that your kid has soccer tournaments. You know that you'll want to go out to eat during the weekend. You know that you'll buy a new nail polish at the drugstore. You know that you'll invite a friend over for cocktails. You know this because it's your life.

And this is what you must truly budget for. This system is not about pinching pennies; it's about strategizing the ones you've got, in such a way that maximizes the joy of living.

We are conscious of the many things that seem to derail our budget. It's the weddings. It's the birthday parties our kids go to. It's a date night with the spouse. It's having friends over for a game night. We know about these events; we just don't set a plan in our budget to pay for them. And then the excuse we offer is "Well, couldn't have planned for that!"

Buuuuut, you can—and that's what I hope my system helps you do.

Even if you pride yourself on your spontaneity, I challenge you to write down the kinds of events you're spontaneous about. You *can* budget for a last-minute camping trip or an out-of-the-blue dinner date. You *can* be financially prepared for the unexpected, as long as you're thoughtful enough about the way you actually live (and want to live).

Life is about so much more than just paying the bills. Let's make sure your budget reflects that.

Make It Happen

Draw or print out a calendar for the next twelve months.

List all holidays and onetime events you have planned.

List all annual and semiannual expenses, placing them on their due date.

Take the three months ahead of you and focus on those: What normal life events can you expect soon?

List all paydays as well as fixed and variable expenses for the next three months.

Try the highlighter method: Which paychecks cover your expenses?

For Those Following along with the Budget by Paycheck Method

Go to Steps #3 and #5: Identify your regular bills or fixed expenses. Fill out your budget calendar.

CHAPTER EIGHT

Avoid Budget Burnout

Shonya, a forty-seven-year-old life empowerment coach, has worked tirelessly alongside her husband of twenty-seven years to create a beautiful home for their three daughters. Neither are strangers to hard work; both have always taken any available overtime they could get their hands on while simultaneously starting a number of side hustles for extra cash. As the budgeter of her household, her mindset became hustle, then spend.

There was only one problem: no matter how much cash she and her husband brought in, it was never enough. She was drowning in debt. She began seeking the wisdom of experts on blogs, books, and podcasts, and decided she needed to start putting every penny toward her debt, adopting a strict "rice and beans" money mentality. She learned that the first step was saving $1,000 in an emergency fund, but every time she accomplished that, life would happen. A birthday would come out of nowhere, her tires would need to be replaced, or the brakes in her car would give out. (Fortunately, that only happened once.) Not only would she deplete the savings she'd worked so hard to accumulate on these surprise expenses, but she would use her credit cards to cover the difference.

Then, one day in 2019, just weeks before Christmas while she was recovering from a broken ankle, the worst-case scenario happened: her six-year-old furnace blew. It would cost $7,000 to replace, but she had no extra savings to cover the bill. The conventional financial wisdom she'd been following told her that she had no other choice but to sell her home, but she just couldn't bear the thought.

Instead, she borrowed $7,000 from her husband's grandfather—something every bone in her body resisted—to fix the furnace. Along with the loan came an immense feeling of guilt, so she hustled even harder to pay him back at lightning speed. But in the meantime, while she paid back the loan, she was forced to rely on her credit cards once again. The debt continued to accumulate. She vowed never to put herself or her husband in such a position of vulnerability again, so she tightened her purse strings even more and adopted a total deprivation approach (sort of like being on a strict, no-nonsense diet). She found herself delaying happiness until she "lost the weight." There was only one problem:

It was unsustainable. There was no room for her or her family in this equation. She felt trapped.

Shonya found the Budget Mom YouTube channel in May of 2020. She felt like she could relate to my posts because we both were motivated by wanting to create the best possible life for our families. She spent the first month of the program doing something she'd never done before: tracking every single one of her expenses—including the real-life ones that brought her joy. With her always-frugal husband as her biggest cheerleader, she began with a goal of paying every bill she had using the *previous* month's income. Within a month of using the Budget by Paycheck Method, she met this goal and was able to pay all of her bills, focusing on her credit card bills, before they were due. And she even stopped binge spending over the weekend to make up for all the deprivation during the week . . . because she wasn't deprived.

That's when Shonya experienced the big paradigm shift that you will, too: A budget does not confine you. A budget takes care of you! It doesn't restrict freedom or keep you "in prison." It gives you choices and control.

Shonya realized that the key to her success was prioritizing her and her family's unique lives. Before, she stressed constantly about how she would celebrate the events that were important to her, like birthdays, and make them feel special. Now, she sets cash envelopes aside for all of those things, accounting for all of the possible surprises she knows will come up: fall flowers, backyard fun, Fourth of July, Christmas, car maintenance, home decor, home improvements, birthdays, Toby the dog, Costco, and miscellaneous spending. Even her sixteen-year-old daughter has started using the cash envelope system to save for a car.

Fast-forward to today, and Shonya's paid off $14,000 in credit card debt—eliminating *eleven* cards from her life—and she and her husband have both increased their 401(k) contributions by 3 percent. Even more important, she's achieved the budget confidence she's been searching for, and no longer dreads the sight of her account balance on Monday mornings. Another beneficial side effect of spending in accordance with your values: no guilt hangovers.

Shonya's story is all too familiar; I can still remember feeling like my budget was like a strict parent keeping me at home. I felt confined and trapped. I looked at the activities I liked, and I thought, "I have to give up all of this to be successful with my money. I can't go out with friends. I can't have a date night. I can't buy something on a whim. I have to constantly say no to my son." I thought that's what it meant to budget: I had to give up all these things in my life and live by someone else's priorities.

Turns out, the opposite is true; I just had to learn how to say yes to life in new ways. Being prepared gave me more options, not less. Planning and budgeting ensure you're never backed into a corner and can choose at will. Financial stability gives you peace of mind. Financial stability allows you to do what you value with your money. Financial stability gives you your life back in ways you haven't felt maybe ever.

What really confines us in our lives is the bill we're not prepared for, the emergency that takes precedence over everything else, the increasing debt payments—these trap us, because they make us rearrange our lives and force us to rely even more on debt. Think about how often you feel pressured to use credit instead of cash. Why? We think that credit line is the only option, but, in reality, it's the only option we gave ourselves. And suddenly, we don't have money for what we actually need, much less anything fun.

I remember going to the beach—something I do often in the summer—and every single day when I would step out the door, I would ask myself, "Did I grab my credit card?" I was hypervigilant, always worrying there might be something I'd want to buy but wouldn't have the money for. A credit card was the only option I prepared for myself.

Today, day trips look completely different. I have a specific amount of money set aside for fun activities. I have a fund specifically for things I *didn't* budget for (it's called my miscellaneous budget). I also have a checking account cushion (more on that later) and an emergency fund. If I need or want to buy something unexpected, my budget has provided many ways for me to pay for it without reaching for my credit card.

I designed my Budget by Paycheck Method and the TBM Financial

Foundations to keep you from relying on debt. A budget helps you make calculated sacrifices so that you have money for what you actually care about.

When I started thinking of my budget this way, I was excited about it, and I was motivated to make my budget work for me. Remember, we use budgets to bring us more joy, NOT LESS.

Setting a Realistic Budget

But not all budgets are created equal. To create a budget that truly takes care of us (and doesn't send us backward into debt), we have to be realistic in every sense.

So what does it mean for a budget to be "realistic"? **Well, a realistic budget isn't based on what you *wish or want* to spend; it's based on what you actually spend.**

We've touched on this, but let's talk a little more about what that means.

When we see how much we're spending (and, oftentimes, wasting) on things we don't actually use, like, or need, it's tempting to get ambitious, to cut our clothing budget way back or to imagine that we will fill up our gas tank only once. We think, "I can totally cut $100 out of my grocery category," or, "I can easily put $1,000 of this paycheck toward debt." We get excited; we want to achieve our goals.

But let's not risk a crash-and-burn scene, shall we? For those just starting out, I strongly caution against being overly ambitious. A budget can take care of us only if it's realistic, and it's more difficult to stick to spending goals than we might imagine at first (more on how to keep on track in the next chapter). When we budget unrealistic numbers, we get discouraged, and we don't actually make any progress. We might even be tempted to give up completely—what I call **budget burnout.**

The quickest way to budget burnout is to ignore your real spending patterns when making a budget. People look at a category like "beauty" and think, "Forty dollars sounds right." To those people (and I used to be one of them), I want to ask, "Where are you getting that number?" If they haven't actually looked at what they normally spend, what makes them think forty dollars is right? They'll look at a category like "fun" and say, "Sixty dollars." But do they know how much they spent on that category last month? What kinds of activities are their "fun" activities? How often do they come around?

Guessing is a trap. Just because I wish it would be that way (or thought it should be that way) doesn't mean it is. Unless you look at something real, your budget will never help you.

Using other people's templates is easier than sitting down and doing the hard work ourselves. This kept me stuck for a long time. I'd take templates of other people's budgets off the internet and model my numbers after theirs, thinking, "She can stick to spending forty dollars a month on clothes. Why can't I?," or, "This guy spends sixty dollars on household expenses a month. I guess that's a good amount." What wasn't clicking for me then, however, is the very real fact that I am not her, nor am I him. What if I don't need to spend sixty dollars on household expenses a month? What if I need *more* clothes than she does, because maybe I live in Minnesota and it's extra cold? My needs are different from theirs.

Now, am I saying that $500 a month for a grocery budget is unattainable for the person currently spending $1,000? Not at all. What I'm saying is that when you're just starting this process, knowing what you're currently spending is critical because it allows you to be aware of where you're really starting—not where you wish you were.

For example, when it comes to groceries, by knowing where you're really starting, you can make an achievable decrease in your food budget. You can take small steps like meal planning. You can look up recipes that use food you already have in your pantry or fridge. You can use leftovers. You can buy bulk and freeze. Make meals ahead of time. Take one or two of these small steps and decrease your budget just a little bit. If you can stick to that, great. And then, in your next budget, you can decrease it by another baby step. **Incremental change with doable steps is lasting. That's the difference between a random budget off the internet and a realistic budget custom designed for you.**

This is why TBM Foundation #2 of financial awareness is so important: familiarize yourself with your spending patterns and start there.

Don't get me wrong—it's great to have ambitious goals like paying off credit card debt in a year or increasing your emergency fund by $3,000 in six months. But stretching any budget too thin with unreasonable deadlines will wear you out faster than anything else.

Fortunately, you have everything you need to create a realistic budget. Every foundation you've laid so far builds to this, the creation of your budget. We're going to return to four areas of your budget (you'll recognize these areas by now!), and we're going to assign dollar amounts to each to give us the most financial stability possible. Those four areas, in order, are fixed expenses, variable expenses, savings, and debt payoff.

Fixed Expenses

This is the most straightforward category and the most predictable. Remember, fixed expenses are expenses in your monthly budget that never change (or don't change much). For example, your car payment will always be $250 a month. Your mortgage will always be $1,500 a month.

Even though you might want to pay more than the minimum amount on your debt (more on that in Foundation #7), you'll want to list each minimum payment that you have to make here as well as any automatic contributions to savings or investments.

Add up the total. Your income covers these expenses first.

Variable Expenses

Once all of your necessary bills are accounted for, you need to figure out how much you spend on variable expenses. Remember, a budget isn't created just for your bills. In fact, your budget has the most impact on the spending that changes from month to month.

You set the categories with the highlighter method in TBM Foundation #2: financial awareness. Set a limit for each one based on what you learned from tracking your spending. Look at past spending trends and determine a value for your cash envelopes based on your real spending, but also keep in mind that you'll want to still have money for saving or investing. Remember, you will probably tweak these limits as you go, and you should be updating or looking at these limits every time you update your budget.

Savings

The most important part here is to name your different savings goals and prioritize them for this pay period. For instance, instead of trying to save for everything at once, maybe consider setting aside a few months to focus on building up that emergency fund. Not only will this make achieving your goal easier (which will be a motivational boost), it will also provide you with financial peace and stability in an unpredictable market.

If you want to save for everything simultaneously, then make sure that the timelines for your goals are reasonable for your budget, accounting for unexpected expenses along the way.

Debt Payoff, Retirement, or Investments

Until you track your spending and create a budget, you don't know how much extra money you have to throw at your debt, retirement, or investments. That's why this is the last step. I'll say more about these in the next few TBM Financial Foundations. Until then, just know that whatever you have left can go toward big goals.

How to Build Your Budget

Now that you have all the components in front of you, it's time to do some math. I created a Paycheck Budget Tracker to help me with this step, and I fill it out each time I get paid. But you can do it on your own, too. All it takes is a little organizing.

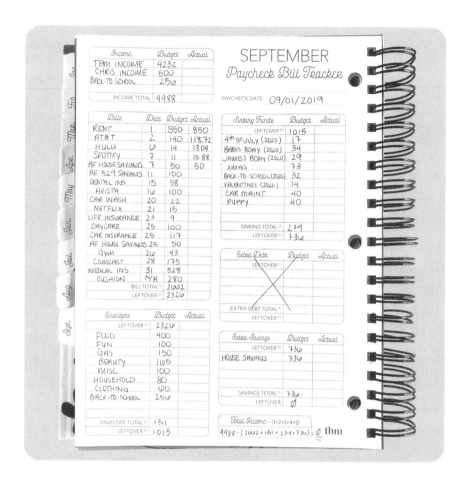

Bear with me, I'm going to get into the details.

Take a look at the expenses you matched with each paycheck on your budget calendar. First, subtract your regular bills (including your minimum debt payments) from your paycheck and then your variable expenses matched with that paycheck.

The income you are receiving should be enough to cover your regular bills and your variable spending. If it doesn't, you have either an income problem or a spending problem. If you can't cover these, something (either expenses or income) needs to change soon. That might mean picking up another job, like Jeanine in chapter 3 did when she began delivering food on Instacart, moving to a place with cheaper rent, re-evaluating your transportation habits (biking or walking to work), or even getting a new job. These changes may sound like a lot, but the alternative (never truly succeeding with your money) is worse.

If you subtract your regular bills and your variable spending from your income and you have money left over, that's when you can make progress on your goals. You can put it toward things in your life that matter most to you, like debt or savings. Remember, this budgeting method isn't just for budgeting; it's an overall financial plan for your money.

For example, let's say your fixed monthly expenses are rent ($700), utilities ($100), food ($150), student loans ($300), and car payment ($300). Assuming a monthly income of $3,000, you would still have $1,450 left over. Next, add up your variable expenses. Let's say those add up to $600. That leaves you $850 to "play" with.

This is where budgeting gets really personal. You have four options with what to do with the rest of this money:

Throw that extra income toward **sinking funds** to prepare for expenses you know are coming up.

Put it toward **debt**. If you are on a debt payoff journey, you might choose to make progress here.

Put it toward **extra savings contributions**. By this, I mean savings goals outside of your sinking funds. For instance, I have a landscaping savings goal. I contribute to this goal only with leftover income. It's not something I contribute to every paycheck (like a specific sinking fund), but it's something I'm slowly working toward when I can.

Invest it. It's important that we keep saving and investing separated; they are not the same. I'll explain more about investing soon—for now, know that it's a fourth option.

It's important to put dollars toward your number one financial goal or priority, whether that be debt or savings. (Look back at the prioritized goals that you established!) But, beyond that, it's not an easy decision. You have to ask, "What am I truly trying to accomplish? And where do I need to throw my dollars in order for me to get there?"

You can save for more than one thing at a time. People often start this journey with the assumption that they have to pick only one priority and put money there, that it's all or nothing. As we talked about before, I disagree. Again, you may be paying off debt while also building an emergency fund. If your number one priority is building an emergency fund, then maybe you put 80 percent of your extra income toward savings and the other 20 percent toward your debt. Or maybe you're saving for retirement! That goal is worth working toward while also saving for other things.

It's also important not to spread yourself too thin; there's a balance between working toward multiple goals and focusing on what's important. This comes down to your own personal definition of success. Like I always say, your budget is unique to you.

Because it's unique, you have to be willing to adjust. Your budget will not stay the same month after month because, guess what? Life changes. In fact, if you try to stick to one budget over and over and over, you will *not* succeed. Your budget will necessarily change when your life changes.

It is important not only to see how you've spent your money recently but also to keep track of how you spend it during the current month as you go. Keep track of your spending throughout the month so you can keep it realistic next month (again, use the highlighter method—back to TBM Foundation #2, financial awareness) to categorize like items. You will go over and under in some categories. That's okay. As I've said before, this doesn't make you a failure. It means that your system (your budget) needs some adjustment. Keeping track allows you to better stick to your plan and, when you spend more or less, course correct for the next paycheck.

If you get to the end of the month and you had to dip into your savings to make ends meet, it might be time to revise your budget. Being in the negative every month is a glaring signal that changes need to be made (more on my powerful tool to make those lifestyle changes in the next chapter).

I can almost guarantee that the first budget you create is NOT the one you will actually use. For me, it took nearly *six months* to find numbers that worked for my budget and life. If your budget is making you more intentional with your money, however, and is giving you signs of progress, then that's a success. It's working.

The more often you review and revise your budget, the more it will take care of you. It will save you again and again. And every single time it does, you will see that your budget isn't there to restrict you; it's there to help you. It's there to save you from going into debt or keep you from making a decision you don't want to make. It's your friend, and your lifeline.

How to Create Stability in Uncertainty

Financial stability—and your realistic budget—is all about being financially prepared, even when your life feels unpredictable. An emergency fund, for example, is a huge step in this direction. But there are lots of other ways you can give yourself options. Here are a few tactics and tips to support your realistic budget.

Use a Zero-Based Budget

To create the most stability possible, you'll want to put every dollar to work. Without intentionally assigning your money, you can easily lose track of how much you have or spend money without considering the consequences. So I always recommend that people use a **zero-based budget**. If you haven't used a zero-based budget before, it's not as scary as it sounds.

Simply put, income – expenses = zero.

This method of budgeting is a strategy where every dollar you earn has a job. When you complete your budget, there should be zero dollars "left over" in your budget. This is why it's called zero based!

For example, if your monthly income is $3,000, then every line item in your budget should add up exactly to $3,000. When using the equation above, this leaves you with zero.

Every dollar must have a plan. Now, this doesn't mean that you should go on a shopping spree to force yourself to spend everything. Instead, a zero-based budget means that you can account for every dollar and make those dollars work for you and direct them to the places you want.

The primary reason this method is excellent for budgeting is that you can track every dollar spent. By assigning a "job" to every dollar, you can fully see your financial picture and make adjustments. It also makes it easier to see if there are any areas where you can cut back on spending.

When I started with a zero-based budget, I was nervous that I would run out of money. Especially because I was (and still am) working with cash, I'd pull out the money and realize that my bank account was getting dangerously close to zero (as it's supposed to). I didn't trust my budget. If this is you, it's natural. I'll talk more about creating a checking account cushion to solve this problem in the next chapter. For now, know that zero based does not mean "no money left," but no money left that's not *budgeted*.

Keep a Miscellaneous Category

In your variable spending, be sure to include a "miscellaneous" category. Very early on, I realized the importance of having a category to take care of unplanned or unexpected expenses between pay periods. That could look like my son coming to me tomorrow and saying, "Mom, I have a birthday party that I forgot to tell you about last week—it's tomorrow." *Well, crap, it's not in my budget to buy a birthday gift.* That's when I use the miscellaneous budget. Or maybe a friend calls me from out of town and says, "Hey, girl, I'll be there tomorrow! Let's go out for dinner!" That dinner wasn't planned in my budget. That's what the miscellaneous budget is there for—so you are not tempted to rely on debt. People often wonder, "If my emergency fund is only there to spend for true emergencies, what do I spend when something comes up unexpectedly that's not an emergency?" The answer is your miscellaneous budget category. This is your backup plan for spending on unexpected expenses between your pay periods. Make sure you budget for your miscellaneous category every time you are paid.

Become an Investigator

You pay your fixed expenses like clockwork. Sometimes when you make a payment, you might think to yourself, "That bill seems high this month," or, "This doesn't look right." But then you get busy and life happens, and all of a sudden, you move on and forget all about it.

Utility, cell phone, and subscription-based companies profit from your busy schedule. They increase their prices incrementally and then bank on the fact that you're too busy to actually take action. If you look at your fixed expenses, I bet you'll find at least one substantially higher in price today than it was when you signed up. This is even more likely if you are a long-term customer.

It's time to spend some dedicated time reviewing and negotiating your fixed expenses. When looking at your fixed expenses, make sure to count not just monthly expenses, but also quarterly, semiannual, and annual expenses.

Now is the time to be an investigator. Gather up all prices, promotions, and advertisements for services that you use: phone, internet, cable, insurance, etc. Once you have gathered your research, set aside about two hours to make phone calls. Look up your customer service representative's contact or find the customer service number. Then, even though daunting, it's as simple as asking for a lower rate. Here are a few examples:

"Hi, I have been a customer for ___ years and I see I am paying ___ for my service. I see you are offering all new customers this lower rate. I would like that new rate as well."

"Hi, I saw that [competitor] is offering [price] for this service. I am thinking about switching unless you can give me a lower rate. Is there anything we can work out?"

Put your negotiating face on. Don't take no for an answer. If they tell you that they are giving you their standard rate, ask to talk to a manager or someone who has the authority to negotiate your rate.

One thing to note: know what you are willing to accept before you go into negotiation. If they don't offer you a lower rate, be prepared to leave.

Create a Morning Routine

Your budget is helpful only if it's accurate and if it gives you a window into the future. I like to review my calendar and budget as often as possible. For me, what works is to keep a fifteen-minute morning routine during the workweek.

The first thing I do (after grabbing a cup of coffee) is sit down at my **budget station,** a desk I have with all my financial materials nearby. I pull up my checking account online. I like to spend a couple of minutes looking at what expenses cleared my bank account and updating my checking account expense tracker so I know where my money is going. I also update my budget calendar. When I pay a regular bill online, I put a check mark next to it. When that bill clears my checking account, I make sure the correct amount has been processed, and then I cross out that bill on my calendar. I also like to track my cash spending at this time.

Then I get on with my day, empowered to make the financial decisions that make sense for me. Your budgeting routine should not take over your life. Keep it short, efficient, and consistent.

Give Yourself Rewards

Another way to keep motivated and on track is to give yourself rewards. Rewarding yourself doesn't mean luxurious, over-the-top purchases. Joy and happiness are not found in the most expensive items. In fact, what I have learned is that pure joy and motivation come from the smallest rewards. Give yourself a **fun budget** to pay for smaller rewards, a budget exclusively for personal spending. There doesn't need to be a lot of cash in the envelope for you to enjoy it. Maybe it's a trip to the salon if you stay under budget in "beauty" for three months. Maybe it's dinner out on the weekend after successfully making meals at home all week. Even five dollars can do the trick. Maybe it's a trip to McDonald's for a Diet Coke on Thursdays at lunch (my favorite treat).

When I share about my one-dollar Diet Coke rewards, many people will say, "Miko, that's not much! You should have given yourself a lot more than that." I don't think those people realize how much those one-dollar Diet Cokes mean to me. I'll never forget the day that I finally trusted myself enough to give myself permission to buy those Cokes. And I did it after paying off $23,000 of credit card debt in one day! But the Diet Coke is what changed everything for me. It brought back feelings of happiness that I'd been missing. I was so used to guilt, and that guilt led to deprivation. If we don't reward ourselves along the way, we will start to resent our finances and our budget.

By now I hope you understand that realistic budgeting does not mean giving up everything that brings us joy. That's not budgeting. Budgeting allows us to spend money on the things that do make us happy, but also to spend in a very smart, prepared way.

Life is stressful enough, but your budget doesn't have to be. If you prepare, your budget will take care of you even when life is crazy. And life *does* get crazy. We still have to talk about the most difficult part of budgeting: sticking to your plan.

Make It Happen

Look at your current schedule and carve out ten to fifteen minutes for a daily meeting with your budget. Mark it on your calendar or add it to your planner. Positive habits are formed from consistent action.

It's time to start constructing your Paycheck Budget.

Income

Fixed Expenses

Income – Fixed Expenses = A

Variable Expenses

A – Variable Expenses = B

If you have money left over after budgeting your fixed and variable expenses, look at your priority goal list. Where do you want to throw your money? Sinking funds, savings, debt, or investing?

For Those Following along with the Budget by Paycheck Method

Go to Steps #8 and #9: Use your budget calendar to fill out the Paycheck Budget Tracker. Tweak and perfect your budget.

CHAPTER NINE

Become an Intentional Spender

Michelle has always hated money. Raised by a single mother in Brooklyn, she and her four siblings learned how to live without cash, relying instead on welfare, food stamps, and credit for necessities, while her mother battled alcoholism and quit many jobs. After a stint in foster care, Michelle and her two sisters moved back in with their mother to find that, while she secured a job at an attorney's office, she still had a running tab at a bar down the street.

When she became an adult, Michelle resolved to give her future children a life that was better than her own. She moved to Pennsylvania to start a family, but when her husband asked for a divorce seven years later, she worried history was repeating itself. As a result of the divorce, she lost her house of five years to foreclosure and was forced to move into a small rental. She was making around $21,000 per year at the time and received little to no child support. She found herself working full time on weekdays and part time every other weekend, all while taking on seasonal work. Even though she was doing everything she could to make ends meet, she felt out of control.

Refusing to give up on her family, she decided to go to college with the hopes of increasing her income down the road. After four years, she graduated with an associate degree in sociology and criminology—an incredibly proud moment—and then went on to meet her current husband, fall in love, and get married. They bought a three-story, five-bedroom home for their blended family of seven children, and everything, for the first time, finally felt right.

And then the car accident happened. Her husband was badly injured. He was no longer able to work his physically demanding job, and their income took a hit. While he began receiving disability payments of $1,200 per month, it was only a fraction of what he and Michelle were used to. Michelle supported their family on her salary of $37,000, took on a second job, and resolved to make it work. And they did.

But you know how this goes, right? There's always *something* lurking around the corner, and in this case, it was the corner of their basement. Black mold was everywhere, and it had spread. This was going to be brutal on their finances.

Insurance covered $10,000, but they were left to cover an additional $7,000 necessary to rebuild two sections. That's when the debt started to snowball. Michelle halted her student loan payments, accumulated more debt on her credit cards, consolidated them into personal loans, and accumulated more credit card debt again. Her $1,550 mortgage payments crushed her every month, so she paid late in order to have enough cash for her other bills. Then, to feel a sense of normalcy, she took vacations she knew she couldn't afford (proof that money is emotional).

She was spiraling.

And yet, a story like Michelle's is one I've heard over and over again: A mom is drained and stressed and overspends in a desperate attempt to break free from her financial anxiety. She is so stressed she decides not to think about money—until she's forced to.

Michelle found *The Budget Mom* in 2017 by chance on Pinterest. After reading my posts on debt, she realized she didn't even know how much debt she had. She found a free, printable debt payoff tracker on my blog. After adding up the numbers, she was stunned. Between her mortgage, loans, and credit cards, she had accumulated over $223,000 in debt.

While the number shocked her, she felt empowered knowing what it was. She and her husband sold their dream home and rented a two-bedroom townhouse, but that wasn't enough; she was still drowning trying to pay old bills. To make things even more challenging, the same week they moved, her husband was fired from a job he had finally managed to secure. They then downsized again.

This is when she got really serious about budgeting and turned more than ever to *The Budget Mom* for advice. Soon, she was able to cut her family's grocery bill down from $800 a month to $450 a month, eliminated unnecessary expenses that weren't even bringing her joy—like thousands of channels on cable—and put all of the extra cash toward past-due payments. Michelle also started using my Half Payment Method, dividing all of her recurring bills in half and setting aside money every two weeks when she got paid.

Things were about to get even more tight, however; her husband's disability checks were ending. So they took a strategic approach and saved the income from those final checks and carried them over into their new budget. Then they downsized for the *third* time. And despite it seeming like their lives were getting "smaller," in reality, the opposite happened. Michelle could finally breathe. It was then that, for the first time in her life, she found herself one full month ahead on all of her bills.

Instead of her debt snowballing, her good habits did; today, she's paid off $182,000 of debt—with only $41,000 to go—and now she saves for goals like vacations in cash. She is not only on the path to retirement with a fully funded 401(k) and pension, but possibly considering home ownership again.

Michelle completely transformed her financial life, and she's also imparted her newfound budget wisdom to her entire family. Her husband, who is now adding $44,000 per year to their household income, actually *saves*. Her youngest son, at only twenty-one years old, just bought his first house. Her middle daughter is almost consumer-debt-free, with only a few thousand to go on her car. And her eldest daughter went through college mostly on scholarships and grants.

In addition to helping family, friends, and coworkers, she's also mentored fifteen women through the Budget Mom Facebook group, helping them either to understand the program or to see their finances differently to make an impact in their own lives.

Michelle, obviously, is awesome. But in the beginning, she struggled like so many women do, spending to de-stress. Spending to check out of reality, to pretend everything is fine and give yourself a "treat." Can you relate? Have you ever pulled out your credit card because you "needed a break"?

I have seen countless tired moms decide they need a mall trip to "reset their minds." But what starts out as an innocent intention to do some window-shopping quickly turns into a $500 purchase on a credit card.

(I mean, how can you resist yet another 20 percent off at Bed Bath & Beyond?)

And then, of course, they get a phone call from their husband who is stranded on the side of the road with a blown tire. Or a notice from their condo association saying a $3,000 special assessment will be coming due. That's when the reality sets back in: maybe they did not need that Mongolian fur backrest and an "As Seen on TV" sock slider. (Which conveniently *does* help you put your socks on so you don't have to bend over, but will likely have you bending over later—to pray or vomit—when you don't have enough money to pay the bills.)

When we're in this strained headspace, we don't even want to think about money—we bury our heads in the sand and try to fool even ourselves into thinking it's fine, it's all *fine*. But you know, deep down, that it's not fine when you don't feel peace, but fear.

Sometimes, the biggest benefit of learning how to budget isn't even money; it's calm.

The Cash Envelope System

What if I told you there's a surefire way to stick to your budget and experience Zen-level calm year-round? What if I told you that you could change your spending habits almost immediately and never overspend again?

Surprise, surprise, there absolutely is a way—but it requires you to spend money in an entirely different format:

One hundred percent in cash.

I know, you're already thinking this sounds . . . logistically complex. But bear with me, because debit cards and credit cards come with a hidden set of challenges most people never realize: spending one dollar feels the same as spending $100. And, wow, is that a problem when you're trying to rein it in. In both of those scenarios, you break out your wallet, swipe the card, and take your receipt. You never physically *see* how much you're spending—for all you know, money comes from an invisible money fairy. Without physically seeing the money leave your hands, you may *feel* like you have endless money in there—and you tend to spend like it, too.

Plastic makes money intangible.

But you need to make it tangible in order to control it.

Because of this, many people have absolutely no idea how much they're actually spending, especially when it comes to variable expenses. Clients come to me, unable to answer basic questions about where their money goes or what category of spending takes the bulk of their paycheck. I was once caught in this trap as well; I had no idea how much money was going where, and swiping a card felt safe, comfortable, and convenient. After all, this is modern society, right? We go cashless!

Au contraire. We're going to take a different approach—at least until you get on your feet. I started using cash envelopes back in 2016, and it was an absolute *game changer* for my budget. Cash spending was the missing piece I needed to make my budget work for me in ways I never imagined. Using physical dollar bills helped me plan ahead and make decisions with my money based on the long-term consequences of my spending.

Remember the spending categories you outlined for yourself in chapter 5? You'll need those for this step. In short, the cash envelope system divides your money into physical envelopes labeled for different variable spending categories of your budget. Every time you want to spend something in the "beauty" category, you take cash out of that envelope. Every time you go to the grocery store, you use cash from your "grocery" envelope. When you use money for your pet, it comes from the "pet" envelope.

That way, you know exactly how much money you can spend, and once the money's gone from the envelope, so is your spending.

This might sound complicated, but it doesn't have to be. If physical envelopes just aren't your thing, that's okay! Many women in the TBM Family have their own interpretations of this method. Some choose to create several checking accounts for different purposes. Some choose to use cash envelopes only for areas where they are prone to impulse buying or overspending—like their "fun" budget or eating out. The idea is not to create a rigid system you can't follow; it's to create a connection to your spending by making that spending *real*.

I will never forget my first trip to the grocery store with my cash envelopes. I filled up my cart, grabbing all the food and treats I normally bought each week. I made it to the checkout line, and the cashier gave me my total cost. I went to pull money from my "grocery" envelope and realized that if I made the purchase, I would be left with only five dollars in my envelope. This changed my way of thinking immediately. I looked down into my cart and saw all of those last-minute impulse items: the twelve-pack of soda, the cookies, the magazine I picked up while I was waiting in line. *Seeing* how much I had to spend forced me to rethink my spending habits.

There's no doubt in my mind that this system challenged me. It made me a planner. I had to anticipate my needs more than ever before. It also made me redefine what were "wants" and "needs" in my life. I had to get honest and make tough choices. It will challenge you, too. When you realize how much cash you actually have to spend, the list of what is "essential" in your life might shrink. The benefit? You'll be able to make the choices you actually want to make with the money you have.

Using this method was one of the biggest aha moments of my budgeting life, helping me stick to my budget in a healthy way, with healthy boundaries—and it changed my habits immediately. I've become a big believer in the cash-only system (I've been a cash-only spender for nine years now). Nothing else has been quite as effective for getting a handle on my variable expenses—the visual aspect is *everything*.

The visibility of the envelope system lets you see exactly how much cash you have left to spend to stay within your income limits. If you stick to your cash envelopes, there is no way you can overspend. When you are forced to reach inside your envelope and hand over bills for your purchases, the concept of money becomes much more apparent. Using the cash envelope system will keep you tuned in to your budget because you will be reminded of it every time you reach into an envelope to pull out money.

People don't overspend because they don't have enough income but because they can't "see" the big picture of their spending. With cash, you feel your spending in a different way. You see the overall consequences of your spending. When you swipe a card, it's hard to see the big picture. Cash confronts you with the long-term effects of your spending. When you see money disappearing before your eyes, you are less likely to spend wastefully. Every dollar really does matter.

Having trouble imagining how it works? Let me walk you through the steps.

The Cash Envelope Steps

If you've done the work throughout the book so far, you know exactly which bills you have, when they're due, and which paycheck covers them. You've also used these fixed expenses to determine how much money you have left for variable expenses. So take your realistic budget out in front of you so you have all the information ready, and let's go.

Step 1: Pay Fixed Expenses Online

A misconception about the cash envelope system is that you use cash for EVERYTHING. But that's not true. You don't need to use cash for fixed expenses. In fact, I encourage you to set up automatic payments if you can. If you tried to pay cash for things like your phone or cable bill, you would be running to the bank every day. It just doesn't make sense. The simpler you can make these essential, fixed payments, the better.

The "cash" part of the cash envelope system is only meant for variable expenses that fluctuate month to month. They're the expenses we have the most control over yet usually know the least about.

But there are exceptions to this rule. You might want to keep your food budget in your checking account, especially if you always order food online. Maybe you want to keep your gas budget in your checking account because you have small children and don't always want to get them out of the car to pay in cash for your gas, for simplicity's sake. Just be sure, as I've mentioned before, to budget for the worst-case scenario for these so you always have enough in your account to cover the cost— even if you fill up your car with gas more than usual one month.

Step 2: Label Envelopes According to Each Variable Expense Spending Category

These envelopes are especially meant for categories where you overspend. These are categories like food, beauty, entertainment, household, sports, car maintenance, etc. For example, I struggle with my food budget. I have started meal planning to help with this issue, but I also created a cash envelope for all of my food purchases to help me with overspending.

When you decide on your variable spending categories, find a few envelopes and label each one with a marker.

If you're like me, you want your budgeting to look pretty. That's why I created cash envelopes with patterns and colors. Sometimes it's the small things that keep you motivated. If color coordination isn't your thing, know that plain envelopes work just as well (as long as you actually use them).

Step 3: Decide When to Pull Out Cash

I like to pull out cash and stuff my envelopes every time I get paid. The amount I pull out is determined by the amount on my Paycheck Budget Tracker. If my budget for food is $400, I pull out $200 cash on the fifteenth and $200 on the twentieth.

Some of my community members will use their first paycheck of every month to stuff their cash envelopes for the entire month, regardless of how many times they get paid. It's easier for them. I usually take my monthly budget amount and divide it by the number of paychecks I will receive that month, giving me an equal amount to spend on variable expenses each paycheck.

But what happens when you get paid five times a month or receive income daily? To simplify your bill-paying process, I suggest choosing two days every month that you designate for paying the bills. Choose which bills you want to pay on which days, and then make a trip to the bank to pull out cash for your envelopes. Doing it this way simplifies your process and ensures that you don't have to go to the bank every few days.

Step 4: Stuff Your Envelopes!

After figuring out when you want to pull out cash for your envelopes, it's time to stuff your envelopes. This is by far one of my favorite days!

Your budget dictates how much cash you need to put in each envelope. For example, if you have budgeted $200 for food, then put $200 in your food envelope. Do the same for each of the different envelope categories you have created. Add up the total in cash that you need to fund all of your envelopes, go to the bank, and make a cash withdrawal.

Step 5: Only Use the Cash In Each Envelope for That Specific Category

This is an essential part of the cash envelope system! The whole point of planning and going to the bank and dealing with cash and coins is that you get live updates on what you're spending and how much you have left. It's possible to have that tangible connection to the money you spend.

Many TBM Family members have asked me if I ever "steal" from one envelope if I run out of money in another. My answer is "yes and no." The problem with stealing from one envelope when you run out of cash in another is that you will likely not have enough money left in the envelope you're stealing from until you stuff your envelopes again. The only time I will steal from another envelope is when I know I will have enough money in the envelope I am stealing from to get me to my next paycheck.

If you find yourself stealing from other envelopes to cover your food expenses, for example, you might want to rethink how much you are allocating to your "food" category. This is a clear sign that your budget is not realistic and you should think about adjusting that category.

As I make purchases, I like to keep track of my cash spending as well as update my expense tracker so I can adjust my budget in the future.

It will take trial and error to perfect your system. It will also take time and work to develop discipline. As much as possible, try to use money in the envelopes only for its designated task.

Obstacles to the Cash Envelope System

When people first hear of the cash envelope system, they usually express some kind of resistance. They're not ready to embrace it right away.

You may feel the same way.

I've helped hundreds of thousands of people start using this system, and with the change almost always comes apprehension. Here are the most common questions I hear:

1. How do I share my cash envelope system with a partner?

Using an all-cash budgeting method can be hard to figure out when you are attempting to use it with two people. Once you have your budget created and you know which categories you want to use for your cash envelopes, the next step is figuring out how you want to store or carry your cash so it works for both of you. If you carry the cash with you, how does your partner access the cash when you are not together? If you give some of the money to your partner, how do you divide it?

Here are my suggestions:

One way is to decide who the primary spender is in the relationship. This person carries most of the envelopes, besides a few, which stay at home, for access to both partners. For example, the gas cash envelope might stay home, while the grocery envelope goes with the primary spender.

Another way is to assign certain envelopes to each individual. For example, you give your partner the pet envelope. They are in charge of making sure the animals of the house have everything they need, so it makes sense for them to be in charge of that envelope. Maybe one partner is in charge of the food purchases, so they will be the only one who needs that envelope.

Some decide to make two sets of envelopes and divide the cash in half. You would get half in your set of envelopes, and your partner would get half to carry with them. One of the challenges of this method is making big purchases (which might cost more than half the cash envelope). Planning those big purchases ahead of time solves this issue.

Keep in mind that you can use any percentage you want. If you do most of the spending, but still want to give some cash to your partner, you could split your cash envelopes so you get 90 percent of the cash and they get 10 percent. Maybe you take 80 percent of the cash and your partner gets 20 percent. Talk to your partner and figure out a percentage that makes both of you comfortable.

Every relationship and situation is unique. You have to find a way to use the cash envelope system that makes both of you happy. I give you full permission and encouragement to tweak the system.

2. What if I shop online?

Sometimes, making a purchase online is unavoidable. When I have to make a purchase online, I use my rewards credit card and then transfer the amount from the correct envelope category to an envelope labeled "Online Shopping."

Let me explain. At the beginning of the month, my "online shopping" envelope will be empty. When I purchase something online (usually on Amazon), I pay with my travel rewards credit card that's attached to my PayPal account. After making the purchase, I take money out of the correct category envelope and move it to my "online shopping" envelope. When I go to the bank to pull out cash for my next cash envelopes (usually payday), I deposit the cash from my "online shopping" envelope into my checking account. I then use that money to pay off my travel rewards credit card.

It's an extra step, but it keeps me cash based.

3. What if I really don't want to use cash?

By now, you can see how much I believe in the cash system. But if you just can't bring yourself to do it, there is another way: the cashless solution.

Without physical cash, it is all the more important to track, every single time, what you spend. Use a cashless tracker to track the amount you have left to spend in any given category by looking at the transactions in your bank account every day. A cashless tracker is a small tracker that you carry in your wallet in place of your cash envelope. This is like a check register, but only for one category in your budget. At the top is the total for spending, and below is a list of purchases and a running tally of how much you have left to spend.

How to Make the Cash Envelope System Work

. . . .

While people initially object to the cash envelope system, I've still never seen a more effective way to connect people with their money and rein in their spending. Over and over again, people make more progress than they ever have. One community member says that at sixty-five she is debt-free for the first time, and it is because she started cash-only spending.

I didn't realize how much I stayed motivated by physical things (like seeing cash) until everything I had until my next paycheck was there in front of my face. I remember actually feeling scared at first. I was afraid to spend my cash. In fact, I would swipe my card just so I could keep cash in my envelopes. I was terrified of running out of cash, and that led to overspending and overdraft fees, and my budget was all messed up because I was using my cards and not the cash I had budgeted.

What helped me overcome that fear was realizing that I had a plan for a reason, and I had to trust that plan. I had to step away and give up my control, give in to my budget, and trust that process.

Ready to start trusting your plan? Here are a few tips to help you navigate the tricky parts of this step to a financially fulfilled life.

Tip #1: Don't Carry All of Your Envelopes Everywhere You Go

There is only one envelope I take with me at all times, and that's my miscellaneous envelope. If I have no plans to spend money in certain categories, I leave them in a safe place at home.

This is also great if you are working with a spouse or partner. What happens if your spouse needs to go to the grocery store, but you have the cash envelope? Make sure to leave the main envelopes at home if you are not planning on using them.

Tip #2: Break Down Your Cash

Once you are comfortable with the cash envelope system, it's helpful to think about what types of bills work best for each of your spending categories. For me, it's mentally harder to spend larger bills. It's harder to hand someone a fifty- or a one-hundred-dollar bill instead of a five or ten. Plus, you don't want your cash envelopes to be overflowing with smaller bills.

Tip #3: Build a Checking Account Fallback Cushion

If you are using the cash envelope method, it's common for your checking account balance to get low.

In fact, if you are completing your zero-based budget correctly (every dollar of income allocated to a category in your budget), your checking account balance should be low or almost at zero every month. That's because after all of your bills are paid, the rest of your money should be allocated to one of your cash envelopes, leaving nothing in your checking account.

The one thing that has saved me multiple times is keeping a **checking account fallback cushion**. This "cushion" is an extra $1,000 in my checking account at all times, money that will help if one of my bills (utility bill, etc.) is bigger than what I expected. It keeps me from experiencing overdraft fees and allows me to make online purchases without emptying my bank account. I allocate $280 every paycheck for my checking account cushion, and I never touch it. It sits in my checking account, just in case.

If $1,000 sounds impossible right now, that's okay! Your "cushion" is similar to your emergency fund: it's the amount of money that makes you feel comfortable and that aligns with your lifestyle. I am an all-cash spender, so having a big cushion is helpful for me, especially when I shop online. If you're not an all-cash spender but want to avoid overdraft fees, then a $300 cushion might be all you need.

If at First You Don't Succeed . . .

Keep in mind, when you are just starting out with the cash envelope system, you might feel a little overwhelmed and confused. As with any new habit or change in your life, you may feel uncertain at first and want to give up.

No matter what, keep pressing on! If you fail with your first attempt, that's okay. Keep perfecting your system, keep learning, and don't be afraid to try new things. This step is a true test of your "realistic budget," and it's normal to take a while to figure out what works. It will take time to learn the organization of the system and to find cash amounts for each envelope that actually work for your life.

But one thing will work right away: You'll finally feel a connection to your money! You'll finally see what you're spending on, and you will start to change even without much effort.

Once you get a handle on your day-to-day spending, it's time to gather your courage and take the next step toward bigger financial goals, like debt payoff.

It will take more than envelopes to conquer this hill. But I promise you, you can handle the climb.

Make It Happen

Think about two or three categories in your budget where you have issues with overspending. Create cash envelopes for each of those categories.

The next time you get paid, and after creating your Paycheck Budget Tracker, go to the bank and pull out cash for your envelopes.

When you get home, stuff each envelope with your budget limit for that category.

For Those Following along with the Budget by Paycheck Method

Go to Step #4: Cash envelopes. Identify which variable spending categories you want to create cash envelopes for.

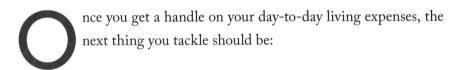

CHAPTER TEN

Defeat Your Debt

Once you get a handle on your day-to-day living expenses, the next thing you tackle should be:

1. Retirement

2. Investments

3. Credit card debt

4. Emergency fund

Can you guess which one of these should take priority over all the others? I'll give you a clue: it's the category you should be the *most* mad about.

It's your credit card debt.

Because even though those little minimum payments feel innocent enough? They're actually stealing your life.

Let's start with the facts. First, high-interest consumer debt is absolutely one of the most dangerous kinds of debt to have, and not just because it represents your love of the Cheesecake Factory. I have met people who accumulate tens of thousands of dollars in debt on store credit cards. No one would consciously go out and put $70,000 on a card all at once, like they would for a home or student loan. Rather, consumer debt is the product of a million little unconscious, spur-of-the-moment decisions, all justified by this one damaging, widespread rationalization:

"If I can afford the minimum payment, I can afford the purchase."

No twelve words have ever been more wrong.

When I first faced the full amount of my own actual debt, I was shocked to discover that I had accumulated $70,000 of it seemingly out of thin air—but I was even more shocked at how fast it had added up . . . without my even realizing. I had seen my minimum payment rising from $20 to $45 to $100, but that's precisely how you get into trouble: $100 didn't feel like *$70,000*. The gravity of that debt was being masked by the only thing I was paying attention to: the monthly payment. That's really all you worry about every month, so it becomes all you see. Minimum payments kept the true amount out of sight and out of mind. I remember feeling so hopeless as I thought, "I'll never dig myself out of this. What's even the point?"

Of course, it got worse. Nine months later, I logged into my student loans to check on my progress, and I almost fell over backward. Last time I'd checked, my student loans tallied up to $32,000. But the number I was looking at on the screen said $33,000. Because of interest and my particular repayment plan, my student loans had actually *increased* instead of decreased, despite my having paid faithfully every month. I actually cried when I saw that. Moments like these can make us feel like trying isn't even worthwhile.

But then I started to feel hints of anger—not at myself, but at my debt. I was losing far more money than I even realized. And when I did the math, it felt enormously unfair. A four-dollar coffee, on credit, would end up costing me closer to ten dollars. Would I ever buy a vanilla latte if it cost ten dollars on the menu? No way! And yet, that's exactly what I was paying . . . not because I was charged that, but because *I* decided that's what it would cost. That was the decision I was making every time I used my credit card.

But maybe what was the most upsetting of all were the opportunities I then had to miss out on because of my debt. I started to wonder, "What would I be doing with my money if I weren't paying thousands of dollars in interest?" Truth was, I'd be doing a lot! I'd travel more; there was so much of the world I wanted to see. I'd work less so I could spend more time with my son. I'd save for retirement. I'd grow more of my money in investments. I'd treat my mom to special experiences. And maybe, just maybe, I'd even own my own home.

Not being able to afford my own home made me especially angry, particularly as my son got older and I wanted more for us. My debt was preventing me from accomplishing what I felt I needed to. I felt like I was stalled out, unable to do anything else until my debt was gone. And I'm not the only one. When I ask the TBM Family what holds them back in life, over and over again the answer is the same: debt. *I want to take a vacation, but I can't because of my debt. I want to save for a car, but I can't because of my debt. I'd like to retire, but I feel like I never will . . .* because of my debt.

The good news is, anger can be exceptionally useful for change. Take a moment to consider this: What's your debt keeping *you* from? What experiences would you have without all of these monthly payments? What goals would you reach for if your money were actually yours to spend?

How to Make a Plan of Attack

Without a plan, you'll feel lost and overwhelmed and want to avoid it altogether. But that's why you're reading this book; we're going to get through this together!

Here are four steps to attack your debt, no matter how large, with strategy and force:

1. Face Your Debt Head-on

You gotta know the real number, the ugly, terrifyingly large $70,000 hiding behind the $100 monthly payments. The very first step is to know exactly what you're fighting so you can come prepared with the right tools. The scariest thing for people who are in debt is seeing that number staring them in the face, but you are going to gather your courage and do the following:

Make a simple list of everything you owe. Write down the balance, the creditor, and the interest rate, along with the due date and minimum payment. You'll find that credit cards and small personal loans have the

OCTOBER
DEBT PAYMENT PLAN

TOTAL DEBTS

CREDITOR	BALANCE	INT. RATE	MIN. PAYMENT	ORDER
STCU CREDIT CARD	$\emptyset$	6.9%	$85	2
CAR LOAN	$16,020.53	3.50%	$349.96	13
DISCOVER CREDIT CARD	$\emptyset$	15.70%	$323.00	1
STUDENT LOAN #1	$10,494.01	6.8%	$35.79	3
STUDENT LOAN #2	$5,114.32	5.6%	$28.59	8
STUDENT LOAN #3	$7,791.17	6.8%	$43.06	4
STUDENT LOAN #4	$100.98	4.23%	$.58	12
STUDENT LOAN #5	$1,797.03	4.23%	$10.24	11
STUDENT LOAN #6	$2,993.98	6.8%	$16.81	5
STUDENT LOAN #7	$1,447.00	4.23%	$8.25	10
STUDENT LOAN #8	$1,079.11	6.8%	$3.77	6
STUDENT LOAN #9	$3,043.18	4.5%	$17.27	9
STUDENT LOAN #10	$4,747.02	6.8%	$26.13	7
TOTAL:	$50,235.53		$948.15	

EXTRA DEBT PAYMENTS

CREDITOR	EXTRA PYMT AMT	PYMT DATE
DISCOVER	$2,821.40	10/9/18
STCU CREDIT CARD	$3,994.84	10/9/18

TOTAL DEBT PAYMENTS IN
OCTOBER
(MINIMUM + EXTRA)

$7,764.39

MONTHLY DEBT PROGRESS

LAST MONTH TOTAL DEBT BALANCE	(A)	$57,541.71
THIS MONTH TOTAL DEBT BALANCE	(B)	$50,235.53
❶ TOTAL DEBT MONTHLY PROGRESS ($)	(A - B)	$7,306.18
TOTAL DEBT MONTHLY PROGRESS (%) (move decimal over two places)	(1 / C)	9.45%

OVERALL DEBT PROGRESS

TOTAL DEBT YOU STARTED WITH	(C)	$77,281.29
THIS MONTH TOTAL DEBT BALANCE	(D)	$50,235.53
❷ OVERALL DEBT PROGRESS ($)	(C - D)	$27,045.76
OVERALL DEBT PROGRESS (%) (move decimal over two places)	(2 / C)	34.99%

highest interest rate. This kind of debt grows the fastest, so it's the most dangerous. I like to arrange my debt according to interest rate, from highest to lowest.

Investigate to make sure you're not forgetting anything. It's helpful to get a copy of your credit report, which will list all of your debt obligations from companies that report to all three major credit bureaus (instead of just one, which might not list everything). It can also help to look through past statements. What do you owe?

2. Figure Out Your Debt Priorities

Deciding which debt you want to pay off first is the next huge step. There are a couple of different methods you can use when determining which debt needs to be demolished first. Before I tell you which method I prefer, let's look at what the two methods are.

The Avalanche Method: The Avalanche Method targets the debts with the highest interest rates first, *regardless of the balance*. Once the debt with the highest interest rate is completely paid off, then you use extra funds to tackle the debt with the next highest interest rate on the list. This type of debt repayment plan, also known as debt stacking, allows you to repay your debts in the shortest amount of time and will save you the most money on interest. Because you are saving more in interest, you will be able to pay off your debt more quickly.

For example, let's assume you have three debts you are trying to pay off.

$1,000 credit card debt (annual interest rate = 20 percent)

$5,000 car loan (annual interest rate = 6 percent)

$5,000 credit card debt (annual interest rate = 21 percent)

To make things simple for the example, let's assume the minimum payment for each debt is fifty dollars. If you have a total of $500 every month that you can use to pay down debt, $150 of that would go toward covering your minimum payments. That means you have an extra $350 every month to apply toward actual principal.

With the Avalanche Method, that extra $350 would go toward debt number three, not because it has the highest balance, but because it has the highest interest rate. That means you would be paying a total of $400 ($350 extra funds + $50 minimum payment) toward debt number three until it is completely paid off.

Once debt number three is completely paid off, the extra payment would go toward paying off debt number one, because it has the second highest interest rate. That means you would be paying a total of $450 ($400 extra funds + $50 minimum payment) toward debt number one until it is completely paid off.

Finally, once debt number one is completely paid off, you would then put all $500 toward the last remaining debt, which in this example is debt number two.

The Snowball Method: On the other hand, with the Snowball Method, you pay off debt in order from smallest to largest balance, regardless of interest rate. By paying your smallest balances first, you can get rid of a bunch of your little debts very quickly. This gives you motivation and instant gratification because you immediately see progress. Plus, with all of your little debt gone, when you start to tackle your bigger debts, you will have the extra cash flow to do it.

Ultimately, the method you choose to tackle your debt needs to be based on your own situation and your own preference. If you are the type of person who wants to celebrate short-term victories to inspire you to keep going, then you are the perfect candidate for the Snowball Method. If you are more analytical and saving money along the way is your goal, then the Avalanche Method might be a better choice.

There is not one right way. As an analytical person by nature, I prefer the Avalanche Method. I'm motivated by the thought of saving interest in the long run. But both are effective; you just need to pick one and go for it. You can even use a combination of the two methods. Maybe you start with one method and do it that way for six months and then try the other.

So, before we move on, go ahead and look at your debt list and prioritize. How will you pay off your debts and in what order?

Once you sit down and make a plan, you will already feel so much better, I promise.

3. Use the Rollover Effect

You can't complete your debt payoff plan until you know how much money you have to throw at it, and you won't know *that* until you track your spending and create a budget. Use your realistic budget (TBM Foundation #5) to determine how much extra money you can put toward your debt each pay period. Continue to make monthly minimum payments, but apply the extra money set aside for debt payoff toward your priority debts.

When you finish paying off your first-priority debt, you can use the money in your budget that had been going to priority number one and put it all toward priority number two, like we just talked about. This is what I call **a rollover effect**. The rollover effect is the most important thing about creating a plan of attack for your debt—even more important than the method that you choose—because it applies across the board. You can use the rollover effect any time you pay off a creditor.

For example, if you were making a minimum payment of fifty dollars every month like the scenario above, once your first priority is paid off, go ahead and apply that minimum payment to your *second*-priority debt. So not only will you be applying the extra money that you calculated in your realistic budget (in the example, $350), but you will also be using the minimum payment amount from the first-priority debt ($50) that you just paid off and the minimum payment you were already paying

($50). That's a total of $450 now going toward your second-priority debt. *That's* the rollover effect. And your goal is to complete this process until all of your debt is paid off. (I promise, it works!)

4. Update and Inspect

It's never enough to simply put your plan into action and forget about it. You have to revisit your debt payoff plan regularly. It can take years to pay off bigger debts, so making sure your plan changes with your circumstances is important. If your income changes, your budget needs to be updated as well. Make sure to revisit your plan as you continue to make payments.

Don't beat yourself up if you make mistakes or get discouraged if you run into setbacks. Pick yourself up and continue with your plan as soon as you can. Debt can be overwhelming but having a plan will relieve stress and give you hope.

Use These Tips to Keep Yourself Debt-Free

#1: Create No New Debt

If you or someone you know works in the medical field, you might be familiar with the Hippocratic oath, which famously instructs, "First, do no harm."

This applies to debt payoff, too. While you're paying off debt, don't create more debt. Sometimes it can be in your best interest to consolidate debt—either with an agency or by using one card to pay off other debt. This is one strategy to keep your interest rates low. But this is not the same as creating new debt. I created my budgeting method to help people live without relying on credit. The earlier foundations of prioritization, realistic budgeting, and cash spending will help you resist the temptation to spend more than you make to create more debt.

#2: Don't Dip into Retirement Funds for Debt Payments

This advice seems counter to the point of this chapter. I can hear you thinking, "Didn't you want me to be debt-free I'd be debt-free faster if I used my retirement money."

For me, using retirement money is a hard pass—no ifs, ands, or buts. I never, ever recommend it. This strong opinion comes from my years working in the finance industry and seeing so many people make this mistake. When people take out retirement money to pay off debt, they lose a large percentage (sometimes close to half!) of that money to penalties, taxes, and fees. And for what? For debt they could have paid off on their own in five years. They will never get that growth potential back; they lost it to a debt they could have patiently and consistently paid off.

#3: Negotiate Your Debt

I encouraged you to become an investigator with your bills. The same is true for your debt! You can negotiate with collection agencies. If you can't make your minimum payments, debt collectors are often happy to set up a new payment plan.

Sometimes, you can settle for a lump-sum payment and get an even better deal. Collection agencies buy debts for pennies on the dollar. When you call a debt collector and offer to settle a collection account in one lump sum, you might be able to save as much as 50 percent or more off the debt. (Secrets everyone should know, right?) You can negotiate and come out on top if you're willing to go back and forth a few times to get the best deal possible.

Some of your creditors might also be able to show you where to get help. For instance, more and more hospitals offer financial assistance programs to distraught patients to help them lower their hospital bills.

After my motorcycle accident in 2011, I ended up calling the hospital in desperation. I explained my situation, and they suggested I apply for financial hardship to see if I could get my bill reduced. The hospital went on to actually reduce my medical bill by nearly 80 percent—80 percent!—just by having me fill out an application. Again, sometimes all it takes is an ask.

#4: Resist Lifestyle Inflation

Instead of using the rollover effect, it's tempting to use new money in your budget for something fun or on new expenses.

Even though I had a budget and a plan, once I started paying off my first debts and bringing home a little more money, I wanted to use the "extra funds" on something fun or new. Likely, you'll feel this temptation, too. Suddenly, there's a little extra left over at the end of the month, and you start to fall into old spending patterns. Now you can "afford" to shop for new clothes, go out to lunch, upgrade your phone, get a massage, etc.

But then just as suddenly, there's nothing left over at the end of the month—again.

This is **lifestyle inflation**. We have more, so we spend more. When you live like this, getting ahead is virtually impossible, no matter HOW much money you make.

As you get out of debt and advance in your career, it's natural to want to make some changes to the way you live. And there is nothing wrong with this! But what we mistakenly refer to as "quality of life" (brand names, dining out, vacations) is really just an inflated lifestyle. This forces us to live paycheck to paycheck, remain in debt, and stay running on the hamster wheel that's taking us nowhere (sounds like the definition of stress).

True story: nearly 60 percent of the people in the United States aren't able to save $1,000. Even people earning six-figure incomes struggle with this, believe it or not, and lifestyle inflation is the number one reason. There's no plan toward reaching any financial goals. It's all too common to assume there's always more time. So, little by little, the money disappears with nothing to show for it but nicer or more things.

When *you* find "extra" money in your account, my smart, money-savvy maven—whether from the absence of a debt you just paid off or even a raise you get at work—you're going to be strategic with what you do with it. Instead of inflating your lifestyle, try increasing your contributions to the things that really matter to you: your hopes, your dreams. Add this excess where you most need it to accomplish not just your financial goals, but your lifestyle ones, too.

Your Grade on Your Debt: Your Credit Score

I can't leave the topic of debt payoff without touching on credit score. The simplest way to think of a credit score is as your "grade" on your debt. If you have a history of struggling with debt (like I do), that might sound terrible. Who likes feeling judged, right? It makes you feel like a kid who just got a bad report card.

But this is actually a really useful metric; it helps you see where to point your compass.

Your credit score measures a couple of important things. For the purposes of illustration, I'm going to talk about your FICO score, which is one type of credit score. It's not the only type, but it's the leading one used by a vast majority of lending decision makers. Here's how it breaks down:

Thirty-five percent of your credit score is based on your payment patterns, or how often you've paid your bills on time.

Thirty percent of your credit score is determined by the amount you owe compared with your credit limit. This category uses a debt or credit utilization ratio: out of the amount of credit you have been given, how much are you using?

Fifteen percent is credit history, or how long you've been handling credit. If you started borrowing at a young age, this will work in your favor.

Ten percent is new credit, which measures how often you apply for new credit.

And the final *10 percent* is what's called a "credit mix," which reflects how you handle different types of credit, like cards and loans.

When it comes to credit scores, higher is most certainly always better. If your credit score is low, don't worry. You can take steps to improve your score.

- **Get a credit report and know what is affecting your score.** You can get a free copy of your credit report every year from each of the three credit reporting agencies. Request a copy at annualcreditreport.com. If you see any inaccurate information, make sure to reach out to that specific agency to have it corrected or removed.

- **Pay all of your bills on time.** Set up automatic bill pay to make paying your bills on time easier.

- **Decrease your debt and keep debt balances low.** The amount of credit you are using makes up 30 percent of your FICO score. To find your credit utilization ratio, divide the total credit you are using (how much you still owe) by the total of all your revolving credit limits (how much you could possibly borrow). I recommend keeping your credit utilization ratio below 20 percent.

- **Open a credit-builder loan.** This is an option not many people know about, and it's great for people starting from scratch or those repairing bad credit history. If you can't get approved for a loan or a credit card, this option does not require good credit. Here's how it works. A credit union gives you a loan at a low interest rate (usually 3 to 4 percent), but there's a catch. You don't actually get the money. Rather, it goes into a savings account for you, you make regular payments, and then, at the end of the loan term, you receive the total amount as a lump sum. You're simultaneously building credit by making on-time payments *and* putting away savings. Neat, huh?

Which Trade-offs Are Worth It?

You already know that my method is all about decreasing your debt while increasing your quality of life. That might seem like a paradox, but as I hope you're seeing, you can be strategic with debt *and* pleasure, all at the same time. You don't have to give up everything to be successful: meals out with friends, new clothes, family vacations, anything that's not necessary for survival. You may think you're being dedicated and diligent, but in the end the restrictiveness backfires. You'll be stressed, feeling guilty at every turn and exhausted by your own efforts. You'll burn out. And worst of all, you won't actually pay off your debt, and then you'll feel miserable while feeling like you failed.

It's not an either-or game; you just need to make thoughtful trade-offs.

We've talked about trade-offs, but they apply even more when it comes to paying off debt. Most people with debt want to pay it off as soon as possible since they feel the weight of it all. But just as important as paying off your debt is figuring out how you can still live your life while doing so.

Let's say a dear friend is getting married in Hawaii, and it would really mean a lot to you to be there. The trip, however, will cost $4,000—a pretty sizable chunk that could otherwise go toward your debt. You have a tough call to make. Look at where that $4,000 would put you if you threw it at your debt: How much closer to your goals would you be? And what will paying off that debt mean for you later? Alternatively, what will you receive if you choose to go to Hawaii instead? You'll need to weigh which trade-off gives you more quality of life. Is it Hawaii with your friends this year, or is it a trip with your family in two? While both would be great, we must make trade-offs to keep our debt-pleasure balance in check.

Trade-offs aren't just important when it comes to big financial decisions; you have to make lots of little decisions with every paycheck. How important are your debt payments compared with other line items? You will see, right in front of you, how much you're spending on variable expenses and how much you're putting toward debt. Increasing one decreases the other.

Learning to manage financial trade-offs is learning to manage your life. You have to weigh what's important to you now while also thinking about your end goal.

If you come up to me and say, "Miko, I really enjoy eating out five times a week, but I also want to pay off debt," that would be a scenario in which you'd need to make some trade-offs in order to have both. If you can reduce your eating out to two times a week and put that additional money toward your debt, you *can* have both. It's just a more balanced ratio between debt and pleasure.

Trade-offs are all about developing self-awareness. You analyze what really brings value to your life versus the habits you've developed in life, and you start making thoughtful exchanges. "I'll trade two happy hours a month this year in exchange for a big wine tasting trip to Napa next year, which I will gift myself once I've paid off this debt." When you start connecting paying off debt with your future goals and dreams, you'll *want* to make your debt payments. It's no longer this intangible, abstract concept you can't see: it's that trip, that house, that car.

Bottom line: do you have to make sacrifices when you're paying off debt? Absolutely. Do you have to give up everything? No. And you're going to decide how much you are willing to give up. It's tempting to ask another person to make these calls for you, but a debt payoff journey is something that no one else can do for you.

When I first started paying off my debt, I saw how much I had been spending on clothes and beauty, and I really wanted to cut back. So much so that I didn't actually buy any new clothes for *an entire year.* I also traded off many of the appointments I once thought I needed: tanning, nails, eyebrows. I gained back hundreds of dollars in my budget each month that way, which I then put toward my debt—not because I had to make myself suffer, but because I decided that those things weren't as important to me as buying a house for my son. In this sense, I wasn't giving anything up, I was GETTING. You see? Trade-offs are all about getting what you want, not giving up what you have.

Other people trade off traveling for a period of time. Others trade off eating out and teach themselves to cook. The key is in having an actual goal in mind for something you want at the end of the rainbow. It's a mistake to try to pay off debt just for the sake of "paying off debt." It's much more motivating when you have a real and tangible vision attached to what paying off your debt will help you GET.

I also kept certain practices that added value to my life, despite their cost. For example, I consistently budgeted for small rewards, like sodas and meals out, if I cooked all week. I also kept yearly vacations on the calendar (paid in all cash). In addition, I continued buying name-brand items whose quality mattered to me, but I did it in a different way. In the past I was the kind of spender who would see a new Patagonia jacket and immediately buy it on my credit card. During my debt payoff, however, I learned to look at all the options with calm and consideration and ask, "Is this worth taking from my checking account cushion or from my miscellaneous cash envelope to pay for it?" Oftentimes, I ended up waiting and saving for it, which made me a patient spender—not to mention someone who knew she could still have what she wanted if she simply planned for it.

When I finally got all the parts in place, and after trying to pay off my debt for years, I was able to pay off $77,281 in only eight months—still one of my proudest achievements. But that's not the biggest sign of my success. After years of paying debt and getting right back into it, I finally addressed the underlying reasons behind my debt. And I finally figured out what my priorities in life were—my son and my family— and connected my debt payoff plan with goals I actually cared about.

Note: Beware of Big Payments

Before we end this chapter, I want to mention a final trap I see when it comes to paying down debt: lump-sum payments.

If you find yourself with a chunk of money, it might be tempting to put it down on your debt right away; that seems like a responsible thing to do, right? And while that *can* be helpful on the surface, I offer a small word of caution: it's common for people to get overexcited, put down a ton of money on their debt . . . and then turn right around and get back into it again. (I would know. I totally did that in the beginning myself.) That's because paying off your debt little by little is actually an exercise in personal development. Remember in the beginning of the book when I said budgeting was personal development in disguise? The best part about paying off debt is the money management skills you gain *while you do it.*

Managing your money isn't about money: It's about growth. It's about consciousness. It's about leveling up. It's about evolving into the 2.0 version of yourself.

And it's about finding pleasure and purpose and passion in a place you least expected.

If you are going to make a big lump-sum payment, analyze your current finances and make sure you won't need some of that money in the near future. I don't think making a lump-sum payment is bad—it's how I paid off my debt—but you need to make sure it won't put you back in debt in the near future. I have some readers who save something from every paycheck to make a lump-sum payment toward debt, and I think that is fine. Just make sure there are no early-payoff penalties.

Make It Happen

Make a debt list, including amount, creditor, and interest rate.

Prioritize: Decide which debt or debts you will pay off first.

For Those Following along with the Budget by Paycheck Method

Go to Step #7: Create a debt payment plan and use the Debt Payment Plan Worksheet to keep track of your progress.

CHAPTER ELEVEN

Begin Your Retirement Journey

R etiring at sixty-five is not the goal.

Financing your dreams *is*.

The book is called *My Money My Way* for a reason: you can't let society tell you what you're supposed to want, when you're supposed to want it, and how much money it's supposed to cost. Just because everyone does something doesn't make it a good idea; it makes it a popular idea.

Here are a few popular ideas about retirement:

- Sixty-five is the ultimate finish line

- That's when you get to stop working

- You're supposed to work hard now so you can play hard later

- But you're probably just going to barely be scraping by

- Because you're also supposed to have started saving for this when you were practically in diapers (but you failed miserably, and now you're worried you'll never be able to retire)

I'd like to offer a fresh perspective on retirement—one you don't hear often, and that is this: *Don't leave the big dreams to the millionaires.*

I say that because there's this real sense of resignation when it comes to retirement; most people started late, if at all, and so the idea of saving, like, *an actual million dollars* feels like WAY too big a stretch. It's formidable. Plus, if you feel like you can barely pay your bills now, how are you supposed to set aside giant gobs of money for a future you aren't even sure you'll be alive for?

I get it. Society has taught us that retirement is a luxury for the rich who can afford it; the rest of us need to suck it up and keep grinding. Many people have pretty much just accepted the "fact" that they'll have to work for the rest of their lives. In the meantime, they're just going to wing it (my famous former move) and hope for the best. They figure social security will save them, their kids will save them, or their part-time job selling tickets at the visitors' center will save them; they'll cross that bridge when they come to it.

Oh, do I hate the phrase "cross that bridge when you come to it." I hate it because it's *not necessary:* You don't have to wing your life and constantly live on the brink. You don't have to forever be on your toes, exhausted, the entire time you're alive. If these hardworking people—these same diligent, dedicated people who are working themselves to the bone—could realize what was possible, they might be able to enjoy their lives now *and* then. They might not be resigned to accepting that retirement is out of their grasp.

The truth is this: you don't have to have lots of extra money, but you do need to have a plan. If you haven't noticed, I don't play by the rules, but I don't have to, because I've got a plan. Having the right plan will let you do whatever you want in life—and you'll be 99 percent ahead of the population who doesn't.

So, let me ask you this: money aside, if you could imagine a world where you *could* retire, what would you want that retirement to look like? What's the craziest thing you could possibly want? What do you aspire to do? Because here's a secret: big dreams aren't for millionaires, *they're for planners*. If you create a plan now, you can make retirement *anything you want*—traveling the world, hanging with your kids, volunteering in the community . . . planting rhododendrons and mixing mint juleps in the yard.

And you don't need to wait until sixty-five. You don't need to wait until your knees give out before you give yourself permission to relax. You don't need to follow the average—and frankly inferior—advice that society offers up as the default option.

You're going to custom create your dream retirement plan instead. And it's going to start with something to which you already know the answer: your *why*.

We talked about your *why* earlier in the book. Maybe your *why* is your kids or your partner. Maybe it's a career or a cause or a certain lifestyle. Maybe it's your people, whoever they are for you. Remember the visuals you attached to your *why*. Bring those to mind (or, better yet, have them in front of you!).

Now, take the visualization further. How does your *why* look during retirement? How have those relationships changed? How are you spending your days? In retirement, what do you do with your time? Where do you live? What do your surroundings look like? How are you contributing to others? What do you enjoy doing yourself?

Dream as big as you can. You have just as much ability to dream as the millionaires do. The only difference is how you get there. Planning for retirement is not just about focusing on the finish line. It's an investment in yourself, in the life you want!

The Path to Confidence: Retirement Basics

. . . .

When it comes to making a retirement plan, there are a few basic questions to ask yourself. Get these questions answered, and watch your confidence grow!

1. How much do I need to save?

If you search the internet with the question "How much do I need to save for retirement?" you'll get too many answers to count. There are lots of different opinions and theories out there about how much you should save, and how much is really enough.

Personally, I use the "25× rule." It's a very simple formula.

Take what you think your annual expenses will be in retirement and multiply it by twenty-five. For example, if you plan on spending $40,000 per year in retirement, then you'll need $1,000,000 to retire. (I know, it still sounds daunting, but bear with me.)

Here's why I recommend using the 25× rule as a minimum goal to shoot for: the rule assumes (using historical market data and inflation data) that you could withdraw 4 percent of your retirement portfolio without running out of money for thirty years.

Of course, you have other outside factors to consider. Inflation, life expectancy, cost of living, early retirement, and market valuations. Remember, we plan for the worst and expect the best. Just like everything else with finances, you have to modify it to your situation. If you, like me, would like to retire early, twenty-five times your annual retirement expenses isn't going to be enough. You'll need to increase that to thirty-five or forty times. Right now I'm on track to retire by the time I'm forty. Adjust according to your goals.

Instead of seeing retirement as a default age—sixty-five—ask yourself what kind of life you want to live in retirement and what that will cost you, and work backward from that to what you need to save for today.

2. Does my workplace offer employer matching?

A 401(k) is a retirement account connected to your place of work, an employer-sponsored retirement account. You can choose to put money directly from your paycheck into this account. This money gets invested in the market and grows with time. Oftentimes, an employer will offer to contribute money to a 401(k), up to a certain amount, depending on how much money you put in. This is called **employer matching**.

Here's an example of what that might look like:

If you designate fifty dollars of your paycheck to go to your 401(k), your employer might throw in another fifty dollars (dollar-to-dollar matching). That's fifty dollars more for you! It's like getting a raise—one that will grow over time through investments. Or they'll do a 50 percent match, meaning they'd put in twenty-five dollars for you.

There's a maximum, of course. Typically, employer matching is promised in percentages. They match a percentage of an employee's contribution up to a certain percentage of their total salary. The most common scenario I've seen provided by employers is a 50 percent match on up to 6 percent of your salary. So, in other words, your employer matches half of whatever you contribute, but they will not put in more than 3 percent of your salary (half of 6 percent). Therefore, to get the maximum amount of the match, you have to invest 6 percent in your 401(k). In this case, even if you put 8 percent or 10 percent of your salary into your 401(k), your employer will still only put 3 percent in, because that's what they've designated as their max. With an annual salary of $100,000, your contribution of 6 percent is $6,000. And your employer's 50 percent match will be $3,000. If you contribute only 3 percent, your employer's 50 percent match will be $1,500. If your salary is $50,000, with the same rules, your contribution over the course of the year will be $3,000 to get the maximum amount from your employer: $1,500.

Many people will argue that it's a good thing to maximize your employer contribution to your 401(k) because you're leaving free money on the table if you don't. And, in many ways, this is true: Who wouldn't want a raise? But it's also about getting compensated in the best way possible for your work and believing that you are truly deserving of that. We need to stop calling it free money and actually look at what it really is, your compensation. Which you are owed. Which is already yours. You just need to learn how to *get* it.

If you have questions about 401(k) or employer matching, connect with your human resources department, if you have one. If not, call your boss!

Contributing enough to maximize your employer contribution is a next step everyone can take.

No matter what your situation is right now, whether you have made major savings goals, or even if you're paying off debt, I recommend taking advantage of employer matching. If it's something available to you, it's an easy first step. If your employer doesn't match your contribution to your 401(k), you can skip this step and move on to assessing all of your investment options.

3. What options do I have outside of my employer-sponsored plan?

The good news is, you have more options than just your employer-sponsored retirement account.

Allow me to introduce you to two main types of retirement accounts: **a traditional IRA and a Roth IRA.** Here, we're not referring to the Irish Republican Army (IRA), but rather an individual retirement account (*that* IRA). They're both retirement accounts you can open on your own, but they have a crucial difference: how and when they are taxed.

A traditional IRA is funded with money that has not been taxed yet (pretax), and it grows tax deferred ("tax delayed"), meaning you do not pay taxes on that money or the growth of that account until you start making withdrawals in retirement (traditional IRA = pay taxes later).

When you contribute to a Roth IRA, your money has already been taxed (after tax), meaning because you paid taxes on the money you already contributed, you won't be taxed again when you take future distributions during retirement (Roth IRA = pay taxes now).

4. Will my taxes be higher or lower in retirement?

Now that you know when the account is taxed, you can compare that with your own situation to figure out which kind of retirement account is best for you. In order to keep as much money as you can, you want to figure out how to pay less in taxes.

And the way to figure that out is by asking yourself, "When will I be in a higher tax bracket? Now, or when I retire?"

The sole advantage of a traditional IRA is that, since it's taxed later, you can take it as a tax write-off now. It makes saving for high earners a no-brainer because the tax savings each year brings down taxable contributions (how much money you pay in taxes every year). However, the tax burden will present itself later in retirement, and will be based on what income bracket you're in *then*—so unless you really need a tax break now, you may want to investigate the Roth IRA instead.

With a Roth IRA, you are operating under the assumption that you're in a lower tax bracket today (and you'll likely be making more money later in your career). If that's true for you, then paying taxes today, instead of later, will save you money in the end. There is no question that the Roth IRA is especially ideal for people early in their careers with salaries in the lower range, given that they have decades to grow their income and most early years of earning a salary come with a lower tax bracket.

Figure out what makes sense for you based on your tax situation.

5. Can I open an HSA?

A health savings account (HSA) is not a retirement account. It is a medical savings account with significant tax advantages. It's like a regular savings account, but the money can be used only for qualified medical expenses. An HSA can usually be used to cover eyeglasses, contact lenses, prescription medications, and obviously, all doctor and hospital visits. It covers all qualified medical expenses without risk of penalty or liability. It can also be used for medical needs not covered by insurance. For example, massage therapy not approved by insurance can be paid for by HSA funds with a doctor's letter stating the treatment is of medical need.

I like to think of an HSA account as the crown jewel of tax-deferred accounts. That's because of its unique triple tax benefits: (1) contributions to an HSA are not taxed now; (2) funds grow tax-free, meaning any growth or earnings through interest are not taxed; (3) distributions for qualified medical expenses aren't taxed, either.

So the question becomes, are you eligible to have an HSA? There are some personal requirements for eligibility: you must be covered by a qualifying high-deductible health plan. When I first thought about opening an HSA, I knew I had a high deductible. Currently mine is set at $6,900. To see if my health plan was a qualifying plan, I made a phone call to my health plan provider. They were able to confirm that my plan was, in fact, qualifying. There are also other restrictions. For example, you can't be enrolled in Medicare (Part A or B) or Medicaid.

If you have the option of contributing to an HSA, I recommend taking advantage of it and adding it into your retirement plan. Here's why: HSA plans help you save on medical expenses, but it also allows pretax money to be invested for retirement needs. Your HSA can actually be invested, and, not only that, when you turn sixty-five, it automatically turns into a traditional IRA. This means that you can literally use those investments for income in retirement, so all the money you think you're saving for health care doesn't go to waste if you don't use it for health care. That's why an HSA can be a valuable retirement strategy; it gives you awesome tax breaks now, helps you cover medical expenses, and, if you don't use it, automatically turns into a retirement account, à la Cinderella at the ball (except instead of turning into a pumpkin, it turns into money . . . much better).

This account was not created for retirement needs, but it ends up helping you because the funds roll over from year to year (and the account stays with you from employer to employer). Even better, your contributions are tax deductible, so your money grows tax-free. And when you spend that money on qualified medical expenses, you avoid tax again. There is currently no other tax-advantaged account out there like a health savings account. Who knew, right?

The downside: not everyone qualifies for an HSA. That's why you'll need to do some digging to find out if you do. But, for those who do qualify, it can be another place to stash cash for retirement (and watch it grow).

6. How much can I legally contribute to this account?

You'll want to find out how much you can legally contribute to any particular retirement account (or HSA), because there are income restrictions and contribution limits. Your age affects this. For example, if you are over the age of fifty at the end of a calendar year, you have access to what are called catch-up contributions. But if you're able to invest young, do it. Investing early for retirement makes such a difference in the long run, you'll want to throw as much money there as you can.

Your Retirement Progression

. . . .

After you ask these questions, you're ready to make your retirement plan, customized just for you. You have everything you need: your goals, the accounts you qualify for, and how much you can put in each one. Now it's time to put it together.

The question I'm always asked at this point is about order: "Where should I put my money first?"

It's true, you don't have endless money, so there needs to be an order of prioritization. Here's my recommendation for how to prioritize:

1. **401(k) (up to your employer match)**
    First, explore employer matching. Get the most you can from the work you're doing now by taking advantage of everything your employer offers.

2. **HSA (up to the max)**
    Next, I recommend putting money in an HSA (if you qualify). As we've discovered, this is basically a magic account that has the best tax advantage (the triple tax advantage), and you'll get to use it on expenses you'd spend anyway (medical), *and* HSA dollars can be invested. Later, whatever you don't use on medical expenses will eventually be available to you in retirement.

3. **Traditional or Roth IRA (up to the max)**
    Next, place money into an IRA, up to the limit you're allowed.

4. And finally, your 401(k) again (up to the max)
Lastly, return to your employer-sponsored retirement account, and max it out.

If this all seems like too much, remember this is a progression. You might not need to get to step four to achieve your retirement goals, and you might not have the funds to do all the steps. There's nothing wrong with that; this is just the sequence I recommend in order to get you the most you can for retirement.

You also, as always, have to manage trade-offs. Maybe you're saving for retirement, but you also want to invest in a goal like your child's education (more on investing in the next chapter). You can put money toward both, as long as you are aware of what you're giving up in the long run. Maybe you're on step three, so you're contributing to a Roth *and* putting money toward the education goal. You have to manage the trade-off.

When it comes to retirement, people often don't think past their employer-sponsored retirement account. Or they max out their Roth IRA and don't know where to go from there. But now you know the tricks of the trade, and which retirement goals you should tackle first in order to win at life . . . The end.

We've covered the important questions to ask as you make a retirement plan and the order of how to progress in your retirement savings.

I want to leave you with a few rules of thumb:

First, use the oxygen mask mentality: Take care of yourself before you take care of others. If you give all of your money away in your early life, you will be depending on others later in life. Remember what your flight attendant says: Put your own oxygen mask on first.

Second, try never to liquidate your retirement assets. Liquidating your retirement assets means turning your investments back into cash you can use, but you lose big when you do that; there are usually giant penalties that erase any interest you earned (not to mention certain rules around withdrawal). In an ideal world, you wouldn't have to withdraw money from a retirement account until you are retired. That's why it's so important to have an emergency fund and learn to save for what you need. And whatever you do, don't withdraw from your retirement account to pay off debt. You will lose much more in the long term than you would gain from paying off your debt early. Only liquidate your retirement assets as a last resort to avoid bankruptcy, and be aware of the kinds of penalties you might face.

And finally, in order to get to that glorious "I've got twenty-five times my income saved for retirement" level, how much of your income should you be saving to get there? Best-case scenario, aim for 10 to 15 percent of your pre-tax income. I encourage you to at least try for that, if you can. But again, as long as you make a plan and manage to save *something*, you don't need to follow any rules. Even if it's five dollars a month. We want you forming good habits, and the amount is far less important than the action.

Make It Happen

Imagine your life in retirement. What does your retirement life look like? Estimate your desired living expenses during retirement.

Income from social security, retirement plans, or pensions should not be included and should be subtracted to get the amount that needs to be funded by your investment portfolio.

What are your retirement goals, and how much do you need to save each year to meet those?

What are your retirement account options? Do you have a 401(k) or another employer-sponsored retirement account?

CHAPTER TWELVE

Invest in Yourself

O nce you have a retirement plan in place and feel confident you're making progress, *then* it's time to look toward your other long-term goals. Your other long-term goals are big, specific goals that will happen before you retire, like buying a house or paying for your child's education.

When we talk about these kinds of long-term goals, we have one major financial tool to help us get there more quickly. It's called investing.

I know that word can be intimidating! When most people hear "investing," they think about all of these terms they see but don't understand: S&P, Dow, Nasdaq. No one knows where to start, and they're overwhelmed. And this fear, insecurity, and overwhelm keeps them from their earning potential. I see it all the time. People will be doing so well with their budgets and paying off debt, and then I mention investing and they completely shut down. "That's beyond me," they say. "I don't know the first thing about investing." And they stop there. "I don't know what to invest in. I don't know enough to start. Investing is scary. I don't make enough money to invest."

Perhaps you feel the same way. But even if you don't feel like you're ready to invest, don't skip this chapter. You might think, "I can't even pay off my credit cards, how am I supposed to start investing?" I've been there, too. I thought, "Why add another thing to my plate!" I felt like it was too much to handle. And worse, I just didn't think I was that "type" of person. I thought, "I'm not 'an investor.' Investors are in big cities wearing suits. Investors are people with money. Investors are already rich." False, false, false, and false.

You don't have to be rich in order to invest. You don't have to be a stock market analyst in order to invest. But you do need to believe that you are a person fully capable of building wealth for your future—and you can figure it out.

All of us have the ability to learn the basic skills of investing. You can empower yourself with information about how the financial world works, even if you aren't ready to start investing just yet. No more saying it's "too complicated" for you to understand. You *can* understand this, and I'm going to teach it to you.

While it's impossible to cover everything about investing in a single chapter (not even close), what I will tell you is this: there are steps you can take today, no matter where you are on your journey, to reach your goals—because that's really what investing is about. It's not about striking it rich or finding just the right company to put your money behind; it's about preparing for the life you want, using tools most people don't even realize they have.

Investing Is a Risk

Investing is the process of buying something (called an asset) that increases in value over time, so when we finally sell it, we make our money back and *then* some. In many ways, it's like having a savings account, except investments grow much, much faster than savings accounts (which is why it's worth it)—BUT, they can also lose money faster, too. That's what makes investing a risk. That's also why I want you to have your other accounts in order first—emergency savings, retirement, etc.—before you approach investing. However, done correctly, investing can be a real multiplier.

Buy low, sell high = capital (that means money) gains

Different investments come with different levels of risk. If you take on more risk, your growth can be faster.

As I mentioned, saving money is not the same as investing money. I've watched people confuse these two over and over. When people treat investing like savings, they put money into an investment account and walk away. But with investing, you have to actually buy an asset and monitor that asset. And you, the investor, are in charge of deciding what that asset will be for you. It's a risk. It's different than just putting money away for use later.

Savings are also easier to access than money you've invested. Your savings are what save you in times of need or when unexpected bills come up. Having six months of savings gives you security. Investments are completely different: They are not for emergencies. They are for long-term goals.

Because you are purchasing something and hoping for return, the investment is a risk. It can be a very smart risk to take (more on that soon), but it's always, always a risk. And because investing is a risk, it's something you need to prepare for.

Do You Have an Investment Base?

People have a lot of questions when it comes to investing. The two most common I hear are: (1) What type of account should I open, and (2) what should I invest in?

Investing is definitely an important way to grow wealth. And, honestly, the more questions you ask, the better. Doing your research is a big part of investing. And a lot of people out there will urge you to invest to grow wealth, so you may be eager to get on it.

And that's great. But the truth is, **not everyone belongs in the stock market**. Just because you want to invest, or just because you're aiming to grow wealth doesn't mean that you are ready to take that action. Before you get into the details of what kind of account to open or what to invest in, it's important to know whether or not you're ready to invest mentally and financially.

Am I saying those people should never invest? *No.* Don't get me wrong, investing is a critical component when it comes to building wealth. I'm saying that you have to have a rock-solid foundation first. That means going through all of the TBM Financial Foundations before starting on this one. This is the final Foundation; it's essential all the other ones are in place first. If you're going to invest, make sure you're ready to do so.

Here's why: when people who aren't ready to invest start investing, they not only will miss out on the great benefits of investing strategically, but also will likely lose money in the process, taking them even further from their goals.

So How Do I Know If I'm Ready to Invest?

I've created an Investment Readiness Assessment, which shows whether you are mentally and financially prepared to invest. If you can't answer YES to every one of these questions, then it's time to take a step back and revisit the previous Financial Foundations in this book.

1. Do I have an emergency fund established?

An emergency fund is cash that is available for quick withdrawals. When it comes to investing, you want to have a safety net in place so you are never forced to liquidate your investment assets in a time of need. Don't invest money you can't afford to lose. Make sure you've got a healthy emergency fund first.

2. Have I paid off all high-interest debt?

The point of investment is to grow your money over time. Historically, the market has produced returns between 9 percent and 11 percent annually over the long term. If you are investing your money *and* paying

16 to 18 percent on high APRs to your creditors, you are losing money, not growing it. Recognize that.

3. Am I meeting my retirement goals?

I recommend investing for goals outside of retirement only after making progress on your retirement sequence. First, go through your retirement progression (see the previous chapter). Only when you put your own oxygen mask on first and feel good about your retirement contributions should you look toward investing for other things.

4. Do I have money to invest?

As I just covered, retirement is a priority before other kinds of investments. But you also have other short-term goals you're working toward—not to mention immediate needs.

Assess whether you have extra money to invest. It doesn't need to be much. You can start investing with as little as fifty dollars every month. If you lay all the previous TBM Financial Foundations first, you'll be able to invest frequently over time with a long-term mindset.

5. Have I identified my preferred investment strategy?

Do you like researching and making active investment decisions for a chance at higher returns? Or would you rather buy an investment that replicates a market's return, sit back, and ride it out for the long term? In the financial sector, we talk about these two ways of investing with the terms **active investing** and **passive investing**. Both have pros and cons, and I recommend researching them more to find out what will work best for you.

As you might guess by the name, **active investing takes a hands-on approach**. If you are an active investor, you sit in the driver's seat to manage your investments, or you hire an active investment manager to make those decisions for you.

Active investors watch their investments closely and make buying and selling decisions based on their own research and intuition. Essentially, they trade when they see an opportunity to make money. This type of investing favors short-term gains, quick turnaround, and quick profit.

This type of investing is beneficial to people who want to try to earn higher returns. Active investing also provides a lot of flexibility to create an investment portfolio (all the places you're investing) that reflects your needs and tax preferences. There are also some drawbacks to active investing. If you are making investing decisions based on your personal judgment and research without a lot of experience, there is more room for error. And if you hire an active investment manager to handle your investments for you, management fees can be very expensive.

Passive investing is more a hands-off approach, favoring long-term financial gain over sporadic short-term profits. Passive investing skips the constant buying and selling and takes a "buy and hold" mentality. It focuses on gradual growth and wealth.

With passive investing, the strategy lies not in buying low and selling high, but in the diversification of your portfolio and low-cost trading in investments like exchange-traded funds (ETFs) or index funds. You know exactly what you get when you're buying because these types of investments replicate a certain index or market.

This strategy can be beneficial if you are looking for an easy and simple approach to investing. It's the strategy I choose because I don't like actively monitoring my investments every day. I also don't like researching investments and then making decisions based solely on my judgment. I don't like trying to time the market for a chance to earn short-term profits. I also like low-cost trading and investing in ETFs. And I like knowing what types of returns I can expect from my investment. Passive funds (like ETFs) are roughly equal to the return on the whole market of their kinds of investments (asset class).

6. Do I know my own risk tolerance?

Risk tolerance is the amount of risk that you are comfortable taking. It's a measure of how much risk you can emotionally withstand. Before making any big decisions, you have to know how much volatility you can handle. Do uncertainty and ups and downs in the market make you want to pull your money out?

For instance, I might handle a 2 percent drop in the stock market just fine. But I might freak out when it drops 10 percent. So I have a risk level that I'm willing to tolerate and a risk level that I'm not willing to tolerate.

As your investments grow, so will your risk tolerance. When you are more secure, you can take some of your money and take bigger risks, but that's only after you're on track for retirement and have the security you need.

Different kinds of accounts also carry different risks:

Cash: Money you have in your bank account, ready to spend.

Bonds: These are invested in a variety of bonds and other kinds of debt instruments, including government,

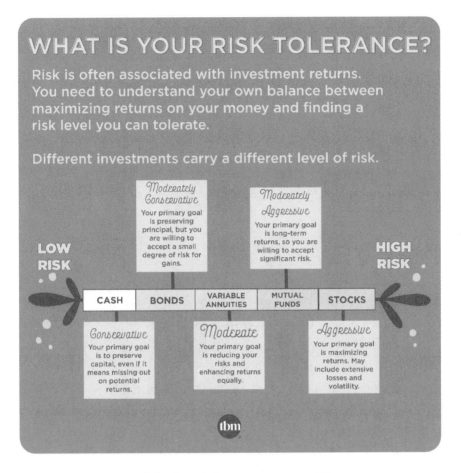

corporate, municipal, and short-term notes. They can also include mortgage-backed securities.

Variable Annuities: This is a type of tax-deferred retirement option (like a contract) that will allow you to choose from a selection of investments. It is an insurance product.

Mutual Funds: Mutual funds are a way of pooling money from a lot of smaller investors to buy stocks in a variety of industries—in other words, mutual funds are **diversified**. Mutual funds are led by professional managers. These managers will be the ones determining what companies to buy and what companies to sell. They involve a wide variety of companies to help minimize risk (to diversify). What people like about mutual funds, other than that they are an easy way to start investing, is that these managers take care of everything! This removes a lot of the guesswork for the investor.

Stocks: Most of the time when people talk about mutual funds, they are referring to stock funds. With stock funds, managers of mutual funds purchase corporate stocks. There are a number of different kinds of stock funds. Growth funds invest in stocks that have a potential for higher financial returns. Income funds invest in stocks that pay a good dividend. Index funds purchase shares of all the companies in a particular market (like the S&P 500) so your returns will match closely to the broader market. And sector funds that focus on specific industries.

These terms may overwhelm you; try not to get bogged down in the details right now. What I want you to see is that each kind of investment is its own kind of risk. You have to know your own risk tolerance and know what you might like to invest in.

No one has a crystal ball, and the market will always fluctuate; that's what it does. That's why I always encourage people to invest for the long term (more on that soon) and know their risk tolerance limit.

7. Have I clarified a time horizon?

Risk capacity is a measure of how much financial risk you can handle—the amount you can financially afford to take. Big goals often require taking big risks. You may decide that you want to make a risky investment, but can you afford to lose it all? To decide, ask yourself: What kind of risk must I be willing to take to reach my goal? What kind of growth (and, consequently, risk) do I need? How much money do I need to invest? Risk capacity works backward from your goals.

Risk tolerance is how much risk you are willing to accept emotionally. Risk capacity is how much financial risk you need to accept to reach a certain financial goal. And at the end of the day, your true risk capacity trumps your risk tolerance.

If your goal is short term, something like two to three years, then the risk capacity will be high (a lot of risk needed to reach the goal soon). Investing probably isn't the best option. With longer-term goals, the risk capacity might become more attainable for you. What kinds of returns would you need to see to attain your goals?

Bottom line, knowing your time horizon will help you identify the level of risk and what investments might be right for you.

Calculate Your Score

Give yourself a grade on these seven questions, with one point for every yes. What did you score? Four out of seven (71 percent)? Six out of seven (86 percent)? How can you get that up to 100 percent?

How to Make a Smart Investment

My investment philosophy is simple: don't make investing complicated. What I mean by that is "invest for the long term and relax." Here's why.

With short-term investments, people ask questions like:

Which stock should I purchase?

Is the market going to crash? Should I pull out now?

With what's happening in politics, what can I expect from my investments?

Short-term investors focus on what's happening right now with the stock market. They are trying to turn a quick profit. They have to "time" the market, which means that they're trying to buy low and sell high. To do *that* is complicated, and it's highly risky. Timing the markets, especially during stock market volatility, can result in panic buying (or panic selling) and irrational decision-making; you watch your savings go up and down, and it's easy to lose a lot of money.

The truth about investing is that long-term investing is most reliable; it relies not on the everyday ups and downs of the market but on the steady incline over time, meaning what's happening right now, whatever's influencing the stock market, really doesn't matter. Because you're in it for the long haul.

You may have heard of **compound interest or the rule of 72**. Compound interest is different from regular interest in that interest grows on the interest. There's a complicated math formula to explain this, but what you need to know is that compound interest grows exponentially, meaning a lot faster than simple interest.

The only real way you can lose with investing is to take out your money too soon. If you know that you're going to be tempted to back out early—that even a slight fluctuation in your account (down $100) will make you pull out your money and liquidate assets—then you're not ready for investing. It's tempting to want to run and remove your risk. You look at the dip. It's terrifying. It might fall even more. You think, "Isn't it better to lose just $100 than $500?"

Resist! It's normal for the market to rise and fall. Long-term investing is a safe bet, and if you can just leave your money there, time will do the work for you.

The market *will* fluctuate. Over the short term, you will gain and lose money. That's why you have an emergency fund at your immediate disposal. That's why you have sinking funds. That's why you've worked so hard to prepare yourself; it's so that you can have the ability to invest money and let it grow.

If this all seems too overwhelming, you can begin your investing journey with a target date index fund. This will allow you to start without being paralyzed by trying to decide what ETF to buy. A target date index fund is one ETF that contains three types of accounts: US stocks, international stocks, and bonds. This investment will automatically rebalance and reallocate as you get older.

So how do you choose a target date index fund? You choose the fund with the name closest to the date you plan to retire. So if you are twenty-five and want to retire at sixty, you would choose the target date index fund with a date close to thirty-five years in the future, so Target Date 2060. All target date funds have a year in their title. This is the easiest way, in my opinion, to get started with investing if you are feeling overwhelmed with deciding what to invest in. You get the diversification and the reallocation as you get older. Just keep in mind, I don't recommend only having this one fund forever. It's not a long-term strategy. But as you begin to learn more about investing, it's a wonderful way to start.

Believe in the Big, Focus on the Small

My biggest fear when it comes to talking about investing is that people will take one small piece of what I say about a certain account or about investment risk, misunderstand it, and then follow it blindly without asking any more questions. It's why I often shy away from this topic on social media, and it's why I give disclaimers often. I want what's best for you, and I can help you with a foundation, but you have to be the one to build.

I say this about all financial experts, including myself: never follow anyone blindly. The biggest gift I can give you is the confidence to go educate yourself more. I cannot emphasize this enough: Your financial situation is unique. Do the research. Ask all your questions. Above all, make it simple for yourself.

I'll leave you with a motto that has helped me with investing: "Believe in the big and focus on the small." Trust in your own ability and then take the next small step.

It's so important to dream big because if we don't trust in our own ability, we will undermine our chances of success from the start. The actions we put into place right now affect that vision. Who we are today shapes who we are in the future. If we give up on the small steps today, we will live out self-fulfilling prophecies: we never believed in our own ability, so we never even tried.

You are capable of more than you give yourself credit for. You have to start by trusting in yourself. Then, take the next small step. Investing doesn't have to be as complicated or intimidating as it might seem right now. There's an endless amount of information to learn, and you don't have to learn it all, just enough to get to the next step. I've outlined simple ways for you to get started. See how learning one concept already increases your money confidence? Then, you can start treating long-term investing like what it actually is—investing in yourself.

I hope you dare to go big with your life and your goals, and I hope your dreams excite you. Maybe they even scare you a little bit. Your dreams should be big enough that you think, "How am I ever going to get *there*?"

You have to trust that you can learn this stuff. I did it—and I knew nothing at the start. More than that, hundreds of thousands of TBM Family members have done the same. I know it is tough to learn new things, but your future is worth it. Your future happiness is worth it. Choose to be a little uncomfortable now to help yourself in the long run. Choose to invest in yourself.

Make It Happen

Have you started your retirement progression?

Did you take the Investment Readiness Assessment? What was your score? Make sure you are at 100 percent before moving into investing outside of retirement.

Take a look at the long-term goals you established (chapter 6). Is investing a good option for any of these goals?

What's one thing you can do today to educate yourself about investing?

CHAPTER THIRTEEN

Live a Life You Love

Stephanie loved her family. But similar to Ashley's story from the beginning of the book, her husband also developed a drinking problem to cope with daily stressors when returning to civilian life after the military. One day, the violence at home reached an apex. She knew her home was no longer a safe place for her and her children.

After her marriage ended, Stephanie inherited nearly $140,000 of combined debt. The divorce was exhausting her; she was willing to take on more debt to end it as quickly as possible. She was tired of fighting.

For years, Stephanie had suffered from migraines—excruciating, unrelenting migraines. But the stress of the divorce made them unbearable. In 2014, she had no choice but to quit her low-paying job. She knew her family needed the money but she couldn't handle the pain. She began collecting unemployment.

Meanwhile, she tried to apply for work, from basic fast-food positions all the way to entry-level HR positions. She was, after all, almost finished with her bachelor's degree in HR management. She was ultimately hired at a call center. For five months, she endured the office's fluorescent lights and constant sitting, but knew there was no way she could hold down this job or any other while the headaches persisted. Finally, on doctor's orders, she had to leave the job.

Now out of work again, she was barely scraping by and was forced to stop making her credit card payments and put her student loans on forbearance. She felt like she was out of options—but she was determined to find work that her health could handle while she advanced toward her career goals. She visited her local WorkSource office for help multiple times with no results, until one day, their ADA representative referred her to a special program for those who were long-term unemployed.

Finally, her life started to change for the better: her mentor in the program hired her to work for them. Given her ultimate goal of working in HR, she finally got her foot in the door.

Even though she was making a steady income, she knew she had to do something about her debt, so she began speaking to a bankruptcy attorney. She was barely scraping by as a single mom of three in one of the highest rental cost markets in the US—and she knew she had to hit reset. After speaking with an attorney, she called a financial counseling service and spoke to someone who told her the only way they could help her was if she managed to pay off some of her debt herself. A strange feeling welled up inside her: She didn't just want to pay off *some* debt. She wanted to go all the way. She wanted this mental and emotional burden gone for good.

If she was going to succeed, she knew she needed some sort of guidance.

She googled "financial budgeting workbooks" and found *The Budget Mom*. She immediately got the free PDF version.

Around that same time, in 2018, she met her now fiancé and knew that for them to have a successful relationship, they both needed a solid financial plan. That meant paying off her debt and truly accounting for where her money went. She'd always kept a budget, but she'd never held herself accountable. She'd never had savings goals in mind. Subconsciously, she'd planned to live with her debt forever.

Discovering her motivation—her *why*—gave her the clarity she needed to meet her goal. Before, she wanted to give up and take the easy way out. But suddenly, she found the confidence to make it happen herself.

She paid off her Treasury offset debts first: the IRS and a Military Star card, which knocked $10,000 off her debt. These debts were the most dangerous, as they could create wage garnishments and were keeping her from getting tax refunds that she was entitled to. Then she decided to tackle her medical debt, which she accumulated while trying to get to the bottom of her migraine issue, by using her 2020 stimulus money. Currently, she's going after her credit card debt. And last, she will pay off her student loans—which, because they went into default and rehabilitation, are already $20,000 lower than they were to start.

Stephanie's not taking any of the usual paths for paying off her debt, which has been knocked down from $135,000 to $101,000. She's not using either the Avalanche Method or the Snowball Method, but rather prioritizing the steps of her debt payoff journey based on their emotional weight and emotional reward. The Treasury offset debt, which can cause debtors' wages to be garnished, created massive stress for her, so that had to be first.

Stephanie's doing her money, her way. The important thing is that she's *doing*. Despite setbacks, despite mistakes, despite failures, she's moving forward. She even introduced her daughter to her budgeting methods—and as a result her daughter is going through her bachelor's program without any student debt.

W e're so used to beating ourselves up for our mistakes, telling ourselves that we're bad people (bad moms, bad wives, bad students, bad professionals). When faced with the fact that we didn't stick to our plan one month, it's tempting for us to think, "I knew I couldn't handle this. I don't know what I'm doing. Why even try?"

I've been there. But let me tell you something: The first budget you create will never work perfectly. It's your first try. Of course you're not going to balance everything or choose just the right limits and allowances for yourself. I can't think of one example when a person made a budget and never had to adjust it.

It reminds me of having a kid. When I had James, I was so overwhelmed. I had no idea what I was doing. I was staying up all night and worrying all day. I felt like I was running in circles trying to get him to eat or sleep or stop crying. I didn't know what to expect or what baby gadgets I needed. Each day seemed to bring something new that I wasn't prepared for: a new tooth or a baby rash or a developmental mark he was "supposed" to have hit. I had no support, and I felt like I couldn't get anything right.

While I was really hard on myself at the time, I can look back at that person and say, *Of course I didn't know what I was doing.* I had never done it before! I had no reason to know. It was my first experience. If I had another baby, it would be a lot different. I'd still make mistakes, but I'd have the experience of having my first baby to give me a lot of insight and wisdom about what to do differently the second time.

Can you look at your financial life that way? As an experiment? When you view it as an experiment, you take away the pressure to get it right the first time around; all you're doing is experimenting with different variables, just like a chemist might. Didn't work that month? Okay, now you know you need to make a change to the formula. It isn't a reflection on your worth as a person; it's merely an ingredient that needs adjusting. And none of this is failure. Failure isn't overspending on a budget category or even using a credit card. True failure happens when we don't use what we learn to help us transform.

The only time we truly "fail" is if we skip the transformation. If we skip the reflection and self-discovery, then it doesn't matter what we do. Even if we follow every guru's "simple steps" to the letter, we won't truly change. It will be action, but not transformation.

Budgeting shouldn't be just writing down numbers without a clear vision of what the numbers are going to help you *do*; that's just picking numbers out of a hat and hoping that they work.

Saving shouldn't be just putting away money without a purpose. When you don't know specifically *why* you're saving, you aren't motivated and lack the self-discipline to do it.

Investing in the stock market shouldn't be done as a default move without understanding your own risk tolerance. I've watched people who have hundreds of thousands of dollars in the stock market lose incredible amounts of money because they didn't understand their own risk tolerance.

Paying off debt shouldn't be about doing it quickly and then getting right back into it after you've paid it off. You've got to deal with the underlying causes of why you're getting into debt in the first place.

It doesn't matter where you start; it matters that you take the lessons to heart. Mistakes actually help us move forward. Say you look at your budget at the end of the month and see that you spent $1,000 on food. That's a good start, but an even deeper level of awareness is the ability to note *why* you spent that much: "I spent that much money on food because I eat out a lot when I'm stressed. I gravitate toward food as a coping mechanism." That fundamental awareness will allow you to get to the root of the problem and make a deeper change. If you want to spend less on food, it's not about picking an arbitrary number to spend, it's about finding ways to give yourself more pleasure, and less stress, which you'll then see reflected positively in your budget. In this case, your "failure" became the ultimate key to making a better next step.

Perhaps you overspend on your children. Say you look at your spending and realize that a huge portion goes to activities and toys: one weekend it's a trip to the arcade, then dinner out, then you're bringing home new clothes—and suddenly your budget's out of control. Can you ask yourself why you spent haphazardly in the first place? Do you feel guilty for not being able to spend more time with your kids during the week? Do you feel like you're not a good enough parent? Do you feel shame over a divorce?

Shame is a huge spending trigger. When we feel shame—shame about our parenting or what clothes we're wearing or what we can afford on weekends—we're tempted to cave, to buy what we cannot afford to "fit in" or "keep up," or just give ourselves a mental break from worrying about it all so much. We'll do almost anything to avoid shame. This pattern (feel shame, make purchase) keeps us stuck. It holds us back from our true potential by preventing us from saving for what actually brings us joy—not the random things you're buying as a temporary Band-Aid.

As I've shared, this was one of the most difficult lessons for me to learn. When I overspent on my son (especially right after my divorce), I thought that spending on him would make him happy. What I didn't realize was that the money I spent was far more about my feelings about *myself*. I felt shame about a lot of things. But I wasn't actually paying attention to what my son wanted. More than expensive gadgets or a new bedspread or another toy, my son wanted to spend time with me. He wanted my attention. And guess what? That's all free. I had to let go of my idea that "a good mother buys her son expensive toys" in order to get back on track. As I made that change, I was immediately able to define for myself what being a good mother to my son really meant—not merely what it looked like on the surface to everybody else.

My money, my way.

It's also common to overspend when you're out with friends. I found myself in this situation as well. I had a group of girls I hung out with who would invite me out to lunch or to the mall. Whenever I was with them, I felt pressure to spend money to fit in. Eventually I started to ask myself, "If I feel I HAVE to spend money to fit in or have fun around these people, is it the type of relationship that brings value to my life?" I realized the truth that people who care about me will not turn their backs on me just because I couldn't afford what they had or spend money the way they did. I let those friendships go, and I hung on to the ones with people who supported my life. I found I could have just as deep (or better) a connection with a friend on a neighborhood walk as I could over an expensive meal out. What I used to think of as "mistakes" have actually helped me have better relationships.

My life has changed in so many different ways since I started this journey. Not only do I live in a different place, have a different job, and spend my time differently, but I've also changed as a person. I'm more caring, thoughtful, and joyful. I appreciate every moment. I wake up every day and am happy that this is my life. And the greatest benefit of all is I can now afford to support the people I care about, too. It's not about how fancy your house is, if you travel to Europe, or how much you have saved or invested. We're stuck on this idea that wealth is about money. We have an image in our heads that involves fancy cars, big houses, luxurious vacations, designer clothing, expensive restaurants. Maybe we think of millionaires and movie stars. Maybe we think of owning a big home or retiring early.

But none of that is financial fulfillment.

The biggest marker of a financially fulfilled life is a person's ability to give their time, focus, and energy generously to those they love.

True financial fulfillment has nothing to do with how much money you have or make.

Financial Stability

True financial fulfillment is about financial stability. When you reach financial stability, you have options. You are no longer forced to rely on credit, because you plan for your expenses, and you have an emergency fund for the expenses you can't anticipate. Never again will your circumstances back you into a corner.

Even on days you don't face anything unexpected, you'll still have options. You'll be able to choose whether to save or spend, reward yourself, or put money toward the future. You'll see the trade-offs, and you'll have the freedom to choose what benefits your life the most.

Financial Clarity

True financial fulfillment is also about clarity. Not only will you have options, but your choices will be clear to you. You'll know what's really important to you. You'll know what you really want. And you'll know and be able to control the emotions behind your spending decisions.

With financial clarity, you'll know what actually makes you happy versus when you're acting out of insecurity, fear, or comparison.

Once you experience clarity, a lot of needless comparison stops. All of a sudden, it doesn't really matter what choices others are making: you have a game plan, you have a road map, you have a goal, you have a destination.

Financial Confidence

True financial fulfillment is about confidence. Yes, personal transformation brings financial transformation. But the reverse is also true; financial transformation brings personal transformation. When you transform your finances, you transform your life. I've seen it over and over again. A life of abundance reinforces trust in yourself.

You no longer have to wonder whether you're qualified to make your own financial decisions. You hold the keys to your financial life. You're in the driver's seat. And you know in your heart that you are the best person for the job, because it's your life.

Stability, clarity, and confidence: *this* is financial fulfillment. With the Financial Foundations we've gone over in this book, you have everything you need to build a life you love—and you can do it your way. And as you do, you will watch as wealth comes to you.

How Wealth Comes to You

To keep tabs on your financial progress, I suggest tracking your net worth. Your **net worth** is simply your assets minus liabilities, what you

JANUARY
MONTHLY NET WORTH TRACKER

DATE OF REVIEW: [1|31|2019]
Ⓐ LAST MONTH'S NET WORTH: [112,451]

ASSETS

ASSET DESCRIPTION	BALANCE
CHECKING ACCOUNT	1702
AF IRD (VACATION)	1309
401(k)	34,400
PERSONAL EMERGENCY	12,502
HOUSE SAVINGS	490
CAR MAINT. SAVINGS	100
2016 JEEP PATRIOT	11,277
2001 HARLEY DAVIDSON	2545
TBM BUSINESS	50,000
BIZ EMERGENCY	20,002
BIZ TAX SAVINGS	26,002
BIZ SAVINGS	5,000

LIABILITIES

LIABILITY DESCRIPTION	BALANCE
NONE	

TOTAL ASSETS $ 104,355
TOTAL LIABILITIES Ø

TOTAL NET WORTH
(TOTAL ASSETS - TOTAL LIABILITIES)

Ⓑ 104,355

LAST MONTH VS THIS MONTH

Ⓒ CHANGE IN DOLLARS	(B - A) + 51,904
CHANGE IN PERCENTAGE (%) (move decimal over two places)	(C / A) + 46 %

own compared with what you *owe*. You want your net worth to grow, and that's just what building wealth does. Consistently checking in on your net worth helps you assess your overall financial health; it's like taking snapshots along your journey.

If you're seeing your net worth grow every month, you're making progress. Either you're increasing your assets (for example, property, businesses, cash, investments) or you're decreasing your liabilities (for example, mortgages, taxes, debt). You're making progress on either one of these sides. It's like a balancing act. If your assets increase and your liabilities decrease, you'll have a higher net worth.

You always want a positive net worth, but there will be some instances where you might have a negative net worth. Having a negative net worth isn't necessarily a bad thing; it just means you have more liabilities than you do assets. For me, this was the case when I was carrying a heavy debt load. As you address debt, take control of your income, and invest, your net worth will grow.

To calculate your net worth, list all of your assets and their value, and then list all of your debts or liabilities and how much you owe for each. Your net worth is calculated by the following formula:

Total Assets – Total Liabilities = Net Worth

If you need help doing this, use my net worth tracker. Knowing where you are will only motivate you.

But there are greater benefits than a bigger net worth. As you go through this process, you'll find that you'll be able to prepare for the future you want while enjoying the life you have today. You'll find that the numbers come more easily because they are not your focus; your *life* is your focus. You'll find you can afford more in the long run. You'll find that you're more content with what you have, too. You'll find that you better appreciate and embrace each moment. You'll be happier. *Isn't that the kind of life we're all after anyway?*

Alongside those changes, you'll experience what I call a **wealth mindset**. As you begin to live a more financially fulfilled life, watch for the following changes in yourself:

A Focus on Value

When spending money, you'll start to gravitate toward quality and long-term value. You'll ask questions like: What will last? What will I cherish for the long haul? What supports my ambitions? What gives me the most time doing what I love?

You will become intentional. You will find yourself eliminating all kinds of activities—even ones that don't cost anything—if they do not align with your vision for your life, replacing them with activities and relationships that do.

A Readiness to Learn

Instead of thinking to yourself, "I could never learn all that," you will find yourself open and curious to know more. Even when you feel overwhelmed, you will find that you believe in your own ability. You will take it step by step. And pretty soon, you'll be way beyond where you were before.

Preparation for Future Risks

You will anticipate future risks and prepare for them. Maybe you want to leave a job you hate to do something you're passionate about. Maybe you'd like to spend more time with your children or to reposition your life. Maybe you want to become a full-time entrepreneur. Maybe you want to leave your partner. Maybe you just want to be able to take a vacation this year instead of saving the money for emergencies.

You will plan for these changes and give yourself opportunities you never thought possible.

A Long-Term View

You'll start to see everything in terms of trade-offs. Instead of mindlessly spending, you'll see everything as an opportunity to prepare for the future. While you still make time for what you love (as I always say, it's important to enjoy the present!), you keep the future in mind as well.

An Ownership of Income and Investments

You'll start to think of yourself as the boss of your own income. You do not see yourself as limited by one employer or one job. You see possibilities.

Are you an investor? Yes, you'll start to see yourself in this light. Even if you're not investing yet, you'll take steps to get there. In every way, you own your wealth and your future.

An Inclination to Provide Value to Others

So many people go to work, they do their job to the best of their ability, and at the end of the day, they leave. There's nothing wrong with this. But watch for the day you shift your focus and ask, "How can I provide the best value to my employer?" This could look several ways. It might mean going above and beyond on a project, helping out on someone else's tasks, or taking new initiative. Your employer compensates based on the value you provide it as a company. You might earn a raise!

You might find this attitude spilling into your personal life. An abundant life overflows. When you live a life of abundance, you're able to give generously from a full cup.

Pouring Out

I was that girl who used to believe in the big fairy tale: I wanted to find a partner who loved me and wanted to get married. I wanted to experience life with someone who would be there for me. We'd have children, and we'd have this big, happy fantasy marriage and family and life. I watched all the Disney princess movies, and I believed that would be my story.

I asked my mom one day how I would know if someone actually loved me. I'll never forget her answer: "You'll know someone loves you when they're able to put your feelings and wants and needs above their own. That's true love."

That conversation stuck with me through the years. Love is purposeful sacrifice. While I learned that the "fairy-tale life" wasn't real, I learned that true love *can* be—a patient and understanding kind of love. It's the kind of love that I want to show to the people in my life: my son, my family, my friends, and of course my mom, the person who first showed it to me. This type of love is something you need to feel for yourself as well, not just for other people. You have to love yourself in this way also.

This vision of love works naturally with the way I view my finances. Everything that I do—the way I manage my money, the way I set a good example with my spending, the way I spend time with my son—is about purposeful sacrifice. It's all about ensuring his quality of life before my own.

For those of you who don't have kids, your financial life still influences others. It may influence your parents, your future partner, or your future children. It may influence your current friends or what kind of people you befriend in the future (turns out, one of the top determining factors of friend groups is financial compatibility). Before I had my son, I used to think about how, if something happened to me, my parents would be saddled with my school debt, for example (because even death doesn't forgive private loans). I knew that would ruin them financially, and that was hard for me to think about. It motivated me to make enough to pay them down.

For me, my *why* has progressed over the years. Now my *why* includes more than just my son. I also want to give back to my mom, a person who sacrificed so much for me and went through so much personally. In 2019, I was able to give my mom $30,000 for a new horse-training arena. With that money, she was able to clear and level some farmland and start the building process. When the construction started, she could barely contain her joy. I can remember her talking about the time she would spend there, training her horse, doing what she loved. I saw the excitement in her eyes when she talked about the future. You can't place a price tag on that look.

Wanting to give that life to my mom played a role in how I financially operate my business. Instead of feeling motivated (and constrained) by the numbers, I am motivated by love. Ultimately, my decision to have a debt-free, cash-only company gave me options. Instead of feeling like I needed to follow the money or only do what made "sense" with the numbers, my Financial Foundations allowed me to freely make decisions based on the life I wanted for myself and my family. Being financially fulfilled allowed me to pour out. Even now, seeing her happy with her horses gives me a reason to save. It has nothing to do with me—it's about my mom.

Even more encouraging than just helping one person, financial fulfillment has the power to make generational ripples. The biggest honor of being a parent is the fact that you become a resource for your child, and not just by answering their questions, but by living your life. You have the privilege and opportunity to set an example for your child, and so the biggest way to help your kids and change the next generation is to help yourself.

If pouring out feels like too big a step for you right now, that's okay. You might start on your financial journey by doing this for yourself. You might think to yourself, "I want to buy these new jeans. I want a new car." You're not being selfish; you're just starting out. It's a perfectly fine place to be, and it will lead you in the right direction.

Think of how a new car affects the people in your life. A new car protects everyone who rides in it, not just you. A reliable car is a mode of transportation to get to a job where your company depends on you and that provides you with a steady income. You might think a car is just about you, but it's not. It's about your employer and your family, too. It might not be obvious at first, but as you start laying these foundations, you will naturally begin to think about others and less about yourself.

And you'll come to value the small moments. As I build a financially fulfilled life, even more than the big gifts I've been able to give, I value the little things. My son smiles when I spend quality time with him. That smile doesn't cost one dollar, but it's worth so much more to me than anything money could buy. My financial resources allow me to take time away from my job to spend time with my son. That's freedom, a blessing, and a privilege.

At the beginning of my journey, I'm sure I saw my son smile when I was with him—but did I notice? I don't think those moments really stood out to me. I'm sure there were so many moments that just passed me by. I didn't take the opportunity to appreciate them. But as I progressed, I began to study my son's face. I began to connect the dots.

I see that if I give up on my journey, then I give up on these small moments that affect someone other than just me. If I give up, I have to go back to working a nine-to-five job, which means less quality time with my son. But I've seen that smile, and it's a big motivator for me not to give up.

As you lay the TBM Financial Foundations, you will start to notice these small, important moments. Write them down! Any time you think to yourself, "This is why I'm doing this!" make a note and post it somewhere you can see.

What's crazy is that I've found that pouring out works in reverse, too. Giving to others benefits my life as well. It naturally happens that way. Wanting to provide a quality life for my son encourages me to make decisions now to improve my entire financial picture. My son motivates me to make those financial decisions and learn to be the best version I can be in that way.

As you give to others, watch as wealth comes back to you. It might be in the form of a promotion, a new opportunity, or simply the happiness of giving. More often than not, I've found that when I give, it comes back around. Our cups are not just full or just empty; they are refillable.

There Is No Finish Line

What I've learned from my own story and from walking alongside so many others is that, at first, all we want is simple answers. We want the plan handed to us. We want the solution to be cut-and-dried. We want to either completely focus on the future or give it all up for the now. We don't want to think or balance. We want simple steps, and, most of all, we want a clear finish line.

I wish I could give you a clear image of a finish line. But that would be robbing you of the truth that there is no finish line.

I remember when I was in huge amounts of debt, I looked at my debt and thought to myself, "Once I get out of debt, then I'll have made it." I thought about how all of my problems would be solved, if only I could get this debt off my plate. I dreamed about how free I would feel, how I'd be able to do what I wanted. My money problems would be *solved*.

Once I did pay off my debt, I found out how wrong I was. I then had new financial goals to tackle: my son's college education and, not least of all, a dream home for both of us. And once we obtained our home, I wanted to decorate and buy furniture (this time using cash!). I wanted to invest more for retirement and buy a better car. While it's exciting to have new goals, it was also disheartening at first; I felt like someone had moved the goalpost farther down the field when I wasn't looking.

While it is true that my debt was holding me back, it isn't true that all I had to do was pay off my debt to be secure and free. Far from it.

As long as you are alive, you will have to deal with money in some way. You will have money to earn, spend, or manage. You will have money to pass on or to give to others. You will have needs, and those needs will cost money. You can't get away from money.

So what you're aiming for isn't a "finish line" but a continual transformation from who you were to who you want to be, and from what your life was to what you want your life to be. You are aiming to learn about yourself, to trust yourself, and to design a life that you truly can enjoy.

Ultimately, **a financially fulfilled life is not about what you have. It's about how you live.** It's about having options. It's about creating opportunity for yourself. It's about planning *and* pleasure. It's about saving *and* spending. It's about maximizing the time you have, using the money you earn.

It's about living well by spending well—not spending less.

Budgeting doesn't mean you have to suffer in order to make it. On the contrary, pleasure is the by-product of responsibility. Make your own pleasure a line item. Budget pleasure into your life, just like you budget your payments. Make living a beautiful life your priority—even if it's in tiny ways. Because none of this ever had anything to do with how much money you make, but how much joy you experience.

Not budgets.

Not numbers.

Not savings accounts.

Not retirement accounts.

Not investments.

Not the 25× rule.

Not a bunch of pretty-colored envelopes decorating your dining room table.

Just happiness—that's the real goal. Work on 25×ing *that*. Use your money and use it well. Be smart. Be thoughtful. Be present. Be intentional. And be *you*. Go for the things *you* want in life. Design a plan for *your* dreams—and then GO FOLLOW THROUGH. Your money will support you when it has direction. That's the real job: figuring out how you want to direct it. How do you want to use money to shape your life? What do you want it to *do* for you? How do you want to use it to honor you? How can you direct it with love and integrity and conviction? How can you put money on your team?

Regardless of your income level or credit card balance—or whether you're sitting in the McDonald's drive-through wondering if you can afford an ice cream cone—you *can* reinvent your money story. You can trust yourself to do it. You can trust your intuition and your emotions. You can trust in the things you want. You can be radically self-assured that you *are* making the right decisions.

Your money will be there to back you up as long as you have the courage to start the conversation. To get to know yourself. To ask hard questions. To follow your heart and be okay with accepting your emotions. To design your budget around the life you want to live.

To do it *your* way.

I believe in you.

Acknowledgments

Writing this book has been a dream come true, and it would not have been possible without the support from my entire team at Penguin Random House. To the beautiful Helen Healey, my editor, thank you for holding my hand through the process of writing my first book and for believing in me even when I doubted myself. I am beyond grateful for my publisher Adrian Zackheim, publicist Tara Gilbride, cover director Jen Heuer, cover photographer Daniel Cochran, managing editor Jessica Regione, and production editor Megan Gerrity. Without this powerhouse team, this book would not exist.

To my entire TBM community, you are the drive behind my passion. The constant support from every member has truly changed my life in the best possible way. Thank you for giving me a family that is so full of love and free from judgment.

To my entire team at *The Budget Mom*, thank you for going above and beyond while I took time away to work on my manuscript. I am constantly inspired by your daily passion to help people. Ryen, you are my rock! Thank you for constantly carrying the torch, being by my side, and for making *The Budget Mom* what it is today.

To my mom, my loudest cheerleader from day one. Thank you for

Acknowledgments

putting up with my late-night phone calls when I needed someone to listen to my doubts, dreams, fears, and goals with this book.

And finally, to my son, who gives me the courage every day to pursue my dreams. Thank you for giving me the power and ability to see a different and better future. I love you more than words, and I hope one day you will use this book to start your own financial journey, in your own unique way.

Index

Index

Index

Index

Index